# APPLICATIONS OF CONTEMPORARY HARMONY

VOLUME I

LORENZO FERRERO

VIOLET ANAMNESIS PUBLICATIONS
SAN DIEGO, CALIFORNIA

Copyright © 2016 by Violet Anamnesis Publications.

All rights reserved. No part of this publication may be reproduced, distributed or transmitted in any form or by any means, including photocopying, recording, or other electronic or mechanical methods, without the prior written permission of the publisher, except in the case of brief quotations embodied in critical reviews and certain other noncommercial uses permitted by copyright law. For permission requests, write to the publisher, addressed "Attention: Permissions Coordinator," at the address below.

Violet Anamnesis Publications
11880 Bernardo Terrace Suite B
San Diego, CA/92128
www.violetanamnesispublications.com

Applications of Contemporary Harmony I / Lorenzo Ferrero —1st ed.
ISBN 978-1-944213-26-8

# Contents

Introduction .................................................................................................................. 10

CHAPTER [1] ................................................................................................................. 1

Diatonic Major Key Functions ...................................................................................... 1

    Diatonic Major Scale Degrees, Chords and their functions ................................... 2

        MAJOR TRIAD: I ............................................................................................. 3

        MINOR TRIAD: IIm ......................................................................................... 3

        DIMINISHED TRIAD: VIIdim ......................................................................... 3

    Diatonic Cadences and basic chord progressions ................................................... 6

    Cadences ................................................................................................................. 10

    IV – V – I Cadence: .................................................................................................. 12

    IIm – V – I Cadence: ................................................................................................ 13

    IV – I Cadence: ........................................................................................................ 14

    Seventh Chords ....................................................................................................... 17

    Inversions ................................................................................................................ 23

    Basic Voice Leading ................................................................................................ 25

    Modes formed out of major scale degrees ............................................................ 28

    Non-Chord tones .................................................................................................... 30

        Passing tones (PT) and suspensions (Sus): .................................................... 32

        Passing tones (PT), suspensions (Sus), Escape tones (ET) and Neighbor tones (NT) ................ 32

        Passing Tones (PT), Neighbor tones (NT) and escape tones (ET) .................. 32

Passing tones (PT), Neighbor tone (NT), Escape Tones (ET), Suspensions (Sus), ........................ 33

Retardations (Ret) and Appoggiaturas (AP): ................................................................. 33

Application: Combining diatonic melodies with diatonic harmonies .............................. 34

# CHAPTER [2] .................................................................................................... 37

## Harmonization 1 - Using only Diatonic Harmony ........................................... 37

### Basic Diatonic Reharmonization ............................................................... 41

#### Diatonic Reharmonization 1: ............................................................ 48

#### Diatonic reharmonization 2: ............................................................. 49

### Reharmonizing with Diatonic Seventh Chords ......................................... 50

# CHAPTER [3] .................................................................................................... 55

## Secondary Dominants ........................................................................................ 55

### Secondary dominant of the second degree (V7/II) ................................. 57

### Secondary dominant of the third degree (V7/III) .................................. 61

### Secondary Dominant of the fourth degree (V7/IV) ............................... 63

### Secondary Dominant of the fifth degree (V7/V) .................................... 65

### Secondary dominant of the sixth degree (V7/VI) .................................. 67

### II-V cadences in secondary dominants .................................................... 70

### V7/II: ............................................................................................................ 71

### V7/III: ........................................................................................................... 72

### V7/IV ............................................................................................................ 73

### V7/V .............................................................................................................. 74

- V7/VI ..................................................................................................................... 75
- Application ............................................................................................................ 78
- Waiting for Tomorrow ................................................................................................... 84
- Guide Tones ............................................................................................................ 85
  - Waiting for Tomorrow ............................................................................................... 88
  - Counterclockwise ................................................................................................... 92

# CHAPTER [4] ............................................................................................................ 97
## Diatonic Minor Harmony ............................................................................................... 97
### Harmonic Functions in A natural minor: ............................................................................. 98
- Tonic minor: ......................................................................................................... 99
- Sub-Dominant minor: .................................................................................................. 99
- Dominant minor: ...................................................................................................... 99

### Harmonic Functions in A Harmonic minor: ........................................................................... 100
### Diatonic functions of A harmonic minor: ........................................................................... 101
- Tonic minor: ........................................................................................................ 101
- Sub-Dominant minor: ................................................................................................. 101
- Dominant Function: .................................................................................................. 101

### Harmonic Functions in A melodic minor: ............................................................................ 102
### Diatonic functions of A melodic minor: ............................................................................ 103
- Tonic minor: ........................................................................................................ 103
- Sub-Dominant 7th function: .......................................................................................... 103
- Sub-dominant function: .............................................................................................. 104

Dominant Function: ................................................................................................... 104

A Natural Minor: ..................................................................................................... 105

A Harmonic Minor: .................................................................................................. 105

A Melodic Minor: ..................................................................................................... 106

Harmonic Functions in C natural minor: ............................................................................ 107

Harmonic Functions in C Harmonic Minor: ........................................................................ 108

Harmonic Functions in C Melodic Minor: .......................................................................... 109

Secondary Dominants and II-V cadences in minor tonality: ................................................. 110

Secondary Dominant of the Second Degree (V7/II): ........................................................... 112

Secondary Dominant of the Flat Three Degree (V7/bIII or bVII7): ....................................... 113

Secondary Dominant of the Fourth Degree (V7/IV): ........................................................... 114

Secondary Dominant of the Fifth Degree (V7/V): ............................................................... 116

Secondary Dominant of the Flat Sixth Degree (V7/bVII): .................................................... 117

Secondary Dominant of the Flat Seventh Degree (V7/bVII or IV7): .................................... 118

# CHAPTER [5] .................................................................................................. 123

Chord extensions 1: Introduction and Basic Application .................................................... 123

Diatonic Natural Tensions ................................................................................................ 123

Introduction to Diatonic chord scale theory ...................................................................... 131

Identifying a chord scale: ............................................................................................ 131

Chord extensions in secondary dominants ....................................................................... 132

**V7 (Primary Dominant)** ............................................................................................. 133

**V7/II** ........................................................................................................................ 133

**V7/III** .................................................................................................................................. 133

**V7/IV** .................................................................................................................................. 134

**V7/V** ................................................................................................................................... 134

**V7/VI** .................................................................................................................................. 135

# CHAPTER [6] ...................................................................................................................... 139

## Harmonization and Reharmonization 2 ........................................................................ 139

# Twinkle, Twinkle .................................................................................................................. 140

### REHARMONIZATION 1 (Diatonic Chords) .................................................................. 141

### REHARMONIZATION 2 (Diatonic chords, chord extensions and acceleration of harmonic rhythm) ........................................................................................................................ 142

### REHARMONIZATION 3 (Diatonic chords, chord extensions, secondary dominants, acceleration of harmonic rhythm) – Includes Analysis: .................................................. 143

### REHARMONIZATION 4 (Diatonic chords, chord extensions, secondary dominants, II-V cadences, acceleration of harmonic rhythm) ........................................................ 144

### REHARMONIZATION 5 (Changing the harmonic direction of the progression) .......... 145

# Jingle Bells .......................................................................................................................... 146

### REHARMONIZATION 1 (Diatonic chord substitutions, addition of seventh chords, chord extensions): ................................................................................................................. 147

### REHARMONIZATION 2 (Diatonic chord substitutions, addition of seventh chords, chord extensions, secondary dominants, II-V cadences): .......................................... 148

### REHARMONIZATION 2 WITH GUIDE TONES ............................................................. 149

# Harmonization Process ....................................................................................................... 150

### How to designate a chord progression to a given song/tune. ....................................... 150

Reharm Waltz ...................................................................................................................152

    A Section (Mainly diatonic harmonization): .............................................................155

    A1 Section (Diatonic Harmonization, inversions, secondary dominants and II-V cadences): ...159

    B Section (Diatonic Harmonization, inversions, secondary dominants and II-V cadences): .....162

    Reharm Waltz .........................................................................................................167

# CHAPTER [7] ........................................................................................................ 171
    Modulation ............................................................................................................. 171

How It Used To Be ..................................................................................................178

Preview and Topics for "Applications of Contemporary Harmony II" ............................182

Some last words for the reader ...............................................................................183

Index .....................................................................................................................184

References ............................................................................................................185

*This book is dedicated to my family who have always supported my musical career and believed in me.*

*Special thanks to Arya Morales for all her constant support, Jan Rivera for the beautiful publishing work, and to all the wonderful mentors and friends that I've encountered throughout my musical career who continue to forge the musician and person I am today.*

# Introduction

Applications of contemporary harmony is a book written with the purpose of understanding how contemporary harmony works and its development. We will start from the most basic subjects, gradually continuing until we reach more advanced topics exemplifying their use in contemporary music, and most importantly this book will show you what to do with all of this information and how to apply it to your own music regardless of which style.

> *Harmony is color. So, in a sense, this book is about giving you a whole palette of colors that you can use to paint melodies, to change the shade of an existing harmonic progression, enhance it, and change its tone so that it provides a more interesting glow.*

Harmony is one of the most ambiguous elements in music, since it's less obvious than melody and rhythm, and harder to identify for a non-musician. However,

> *Harmony has the power to change the mood and give many different personalities to the same melody.*

In each chapter of this book, we will study the direct application of the theory so you can apply the concept directly into your music.

I have been developing new ideas and teaching techniques over the years, and I believe that in music theory, especially when we talk about harmony, you don't really understand the concept until you are able to hear it and identify it. I believe music is different from any other discipline, because it requires an aural understanding. Without it, it is just a combination of letters, dots and symbols. Therefore, it is extremely important to listen to a lot of music in order to relate the theory with what you've already heard, and to translate what you hear in your head into the paper.

What makes this book different from other harmony books is that we will be constantly discussing the function and applications of the theory. We will start at the beginning and explore each new concept thoroughly, learn to apply it right away and use these newly acquired knowledge continuously in the following chapters, providing a continuity that allows the reader to reinforce what they've learnt, while applying the basic concepts into more sophisticated topics, gradually enhancing and diversifying their knowledge while improving their musical skills.

This way, you will be able to apply all the concepts from this book in improvisation and composition, and not only as a harmonic reference.

We will look at original examples that show the most common uses of the topic(s) with a complete harmonic and melodic analysis. This will allow us to create a toolbox of stylistic harmonic references that will serve you as a base to write music, harmonize and reharmonize in any given style, to get a know-how of when to use certain topics and when not to, and to gain the sufficient knowledge to apply the harmonic concepts successfully.

For this first edition, you will need to have a basic understanding of music notation, basic scales intervals and triads in order to get familiarized with the musical language expressed. We will cover basic harmonic topics.

I will also use some of the same melodic examples throughout the book in order to apply the new topics to a melody that you've already seen. This way, you will be able to see how you can apply new harmonic colors to the same melody and how that can add intensity, change the inflection, add brightness or darkness, and even change the intention completely.

# [1] Diatonic Major Key Functions

THE WORD DIATONIC refers to a note or group of notes that belong to a specific key. Therefore, a *diatonic scale* is built upon the Tonic note of the key followed by a combination of diatonic whole-steps and half-steps. By the same formula, a *diatonic phrase* (it can even be a complete piece of music) can be melodic or harmonic, built upon *diatonic* notes.

*The two most frequent modes used in tonal music are the major and minor scales.*

Every major tonality has a *relative minor tonality*, which will always be found a minor third below the major key. They share the same key signature and the exact same scale notes. For example: In the case of C major, the relative minor will be A minor (a minor third interval below Major C). See the image below:

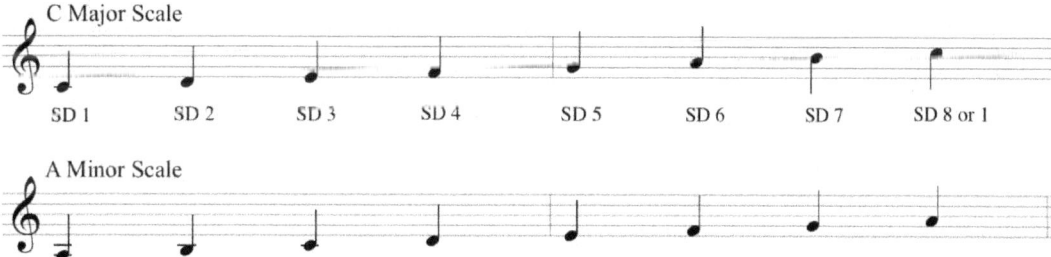

## Diatonic Major Scale Degrees, Chords and their Functions

A diatonic scale degree can be any note belonging to a diatonic scale, which will have a specific melodic and harmonic function relative to the tonality or mode. The scale degrees are the source material for the creation of a melody; they form part of the toolbox that we need in order to generate an organized combination of intervals, which will eventually give us a melodic statement.

For example: Let's take the C Major scale and identify the scale degrees:

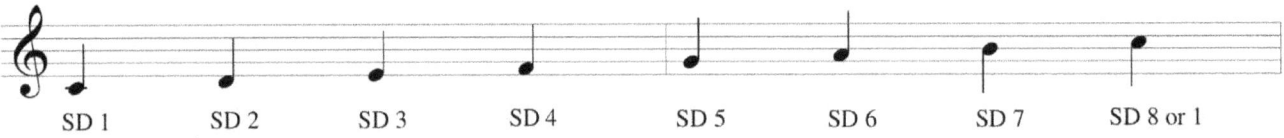

From each scale degree we can build a triad; which is a harmonic structure (Chord) that will give us a harmonic function in relation to the key. A triad is built upon of three notes, which are separated by diatonic thirds (intervals of major and minor thirds accordingly) which when played vertically, gives us a harmony. There are four types of triads: major, minor, augmented and diminished.

When we talk about *diatonic harmony*, we are referring to chords that are built from every diatonic scale degree, giving us a set of diatonic triads that have a particular function to the key. We identify the functions of these chords with roman numerals (I, II, III, & IV respectively). See image below:

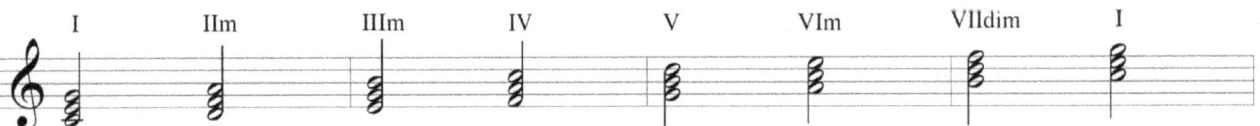

As you can see, a major or minor triad is built out of every scale degree, except for scale degree 7, which forms a diminished triad. The Roman numeral analysis is written correspondingly:

MAJOR TRIAD: I

MINOR TRIAD: IIm

DIMINISHED TRIAD: VIIdim

*Note: Augmented triads do not exist in major diatonic harmony.*

A major triad is constructed by a major third followed by a minor third, while a *minor triad* is constructed by a minor third, followed by a major third:

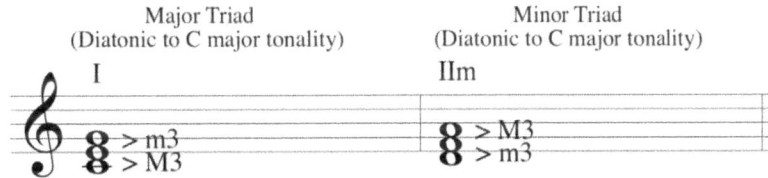

Augmented and diminished triads, on the other hand, are constructed by the same interval; two consecutive major thirds for an augmented triad, and two consecutive minor thirds for a diminished triad:

It is always better to think about the functions first and then figure out the chords corresponding to the tonality. This way, you will develop a functional mentality that will help you manipulate all 12 tonalities the same way.

Now, let's take a look to the same diatonic triads in C major with their corresponding names and functions:

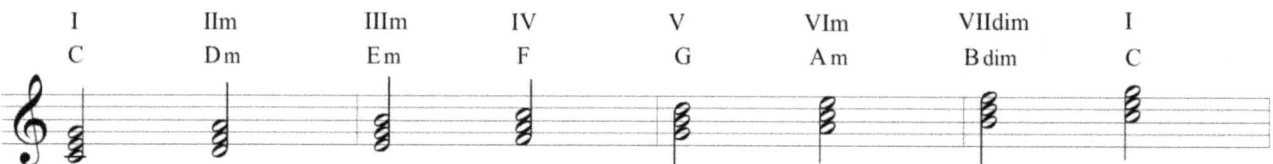

Each one of these diatonic triads has a specific function and sound in relation to the key, but there are three important tonal functions that categorize them all:

> *Tonic Function:* *This is the "home" function. It's the function that represents the tonality and the starting or ending point of a harmonic progression. All of the other harmonic functions have sort of a gravitational pull towards the tonic function.*

The primary chord that represents the tonic function is the I chord = C (In C major), and it is also known as the *Tonic Chord*.

Now, there are also two secondary chords that belong to this function. These are IIIm (Em in C Major) and VIm (Am in C Major). The reason that these chords also belong to the tonic function is that they share two chord-tones with the C major triad, resulting in a very similar sound, therefore serving as replacements for the C major triad.

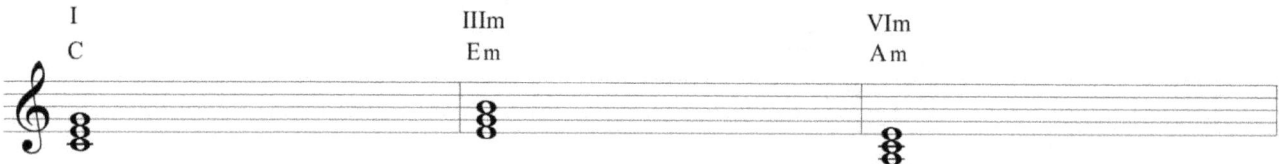

*Sub-Dominant Function:* *This function is known to be the fourth degree of a major or minor tonality. It is called sub-dominant because it is immediately below the dominant and also because it is at the same distance below the tonic as the dominant is above it. The common practice harmonic function of a sub-dominant chord is, like its physical position, to precede the dominant function, thus creating a cadence (which will be discussed further ahead).*

The primary chord that represents the sub-dominant function is the IV chord = F (In C major)

The sub-dominant function, just like the tonic function, also has a secondary chord that represents a similar sound, hence serving as a harmonic replacement. This is the case of the IIm (Dm).

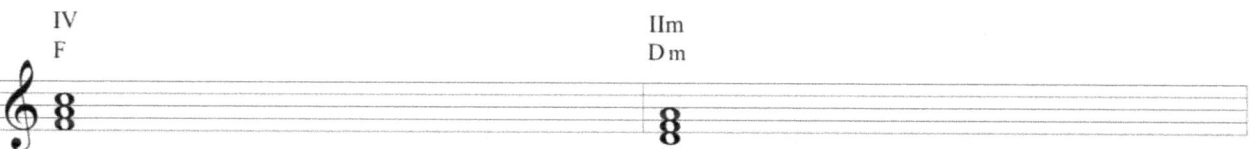

*Dominant Function:* *This is the second most important function (After the tonic) because it establishes the need for a harmonic resolution to the tonic by creating instability and therefore an inconclusive sound. The dominant is always the name for the 5th degree of a given tonality and the chord generated by it (V).*

Primary chord is V = G (In C major)

Secondary V chord is VIIdim (Bdim), which shares almost the same notes, and also creates the same instability and the need for harmonic resolution to the tonic.

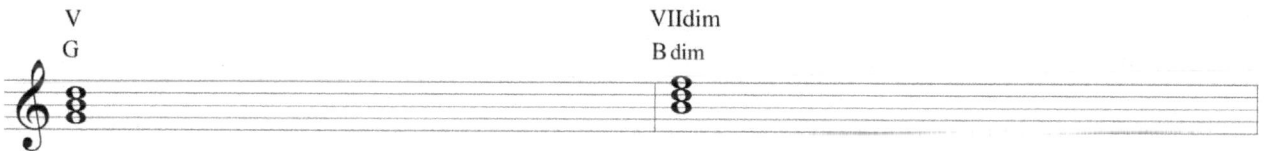

## Diatonic Cadences and basic chord progressions

A chord progression is a sequence of "chord changes" that follow a given musical form and establish a tonality and musical direction.

Let's always consider that harmony is a consequence of musical form. Without form, there is no need for a harmonic progression. This is to say that in tonal music, the chords are not executed randomly; they follow a musical structure by generating harmonic functions and cadences, which have a clear direction. The form can be as complex as a sonata form, AABA, ABAC, or as simple as only 8 measures of music.

In the case of diatonic harmony, we will have chord progressions that go around the three tonal functions that we've talked about: Tonic, Sub-dominant and Dominant.

The following demonstrates a simple 4-measure harmonic progression over a simple diatonic melody in C major using only the primary chords of each of the three tonal functions.

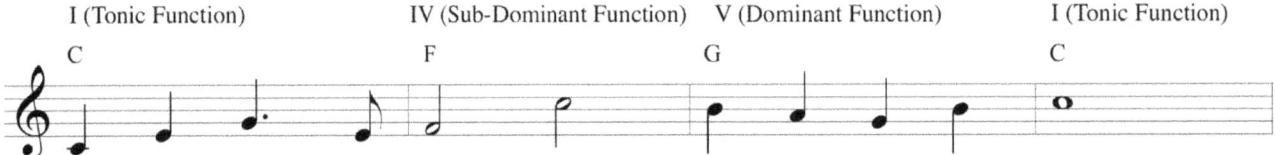

We can see that even though it's just 4 measures of music; there is a clear form and direction generated by the harmonic functions and melody. The first measure starts in the primary chord of the tonic function (C), followed by the primary chord of the sub-dominant function (F) in the second measure, then moving to the dominant function (G) and finally resolving down a fifth to C for the tonic sound again.

In the last two measures of this example, we can see a typical case of dominant to Tonic cadence*.

Also, see how the melody resolves itself by the implication of the notes (see last three notes of the previous image = G-B-C), this is known as a melodic cadence which is effective because of that leading tone "B" moving chromatically to the Tonic "C".

We can see how we only have one chord per measure, which means that the progression has a slow harmonic beat*, creating a lot of harmonic space. We can increase the harmonic beat by introducing more chords per measure, giving much more color and density to the melody. By doing this, we are applying the concept of Reharmonization, which is something that we will talk about in depth later in the book.

*Cadence: *is a melodic or harmonic statement that creates a sense of resolution given either by a set of notes or by at least two chords that will conclude a musical phrase.*

*Harmonic Beat: *Is the harmonic tempo defined by the placement of the chord/s and the amount of chords per measure. E.g.: The greater amount of chords a measure has, the faster the harmonic beat will be.*

How do we do this? We can apply simple reharmonization by adding more diatonic chords per measure, hence increasing the harmonic beat. In this case, it would be a good idea to select the secondary chords that belong to the same function as the chords from the original progression. This way, we will only add more movement, but we will not change the function completely. See image below:

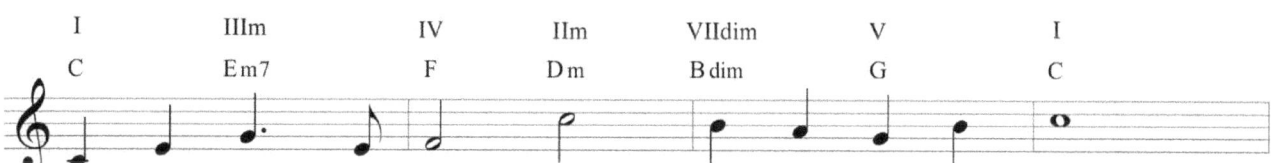

We can see how adding one more chord per measure has increased the harmonic beat. Giving the progression a feeling of acceleration and more density.

It is clear that the first measure belongs to the Tonic function because of the melody and because it is the beginning of the progression. So, I added a secondary chord from the Tonic function in the second half of the measure (Em). This chord gives more movement to the melody, rather than just staying in the C chord for the entire measure. In the second measure, I remained in the Sub-Dominant function and added a Dm (IIm) chord in the second half of the measure. Finally, we can see the VIIdim chord decorating the first half of the next measure before it arrives to the primary Dominant chord to resolve to C.

So, I basically added more color to the progression by placing the secondary diatonic chords in between the melody; creating a faster harmonic beat, as well as more movement.

Now, let's see how these diatonic functions work in a larger musical statement. Let's apply this to a musical period (*). See image below.

*Musical Period: Is a musical statement based on an antecedent phrase, followed by a consequent phrase, each of which begins with the same motif.*

Here we can clearly see a 4 bar antecedent phrase followed by a 4 bar consequent phrase, giving us a period. For both phrases (antecedent and consequent) we start in the Tonic function followed by the Sub-Dominant function, which leads to the Dominant-function and finally resolves to the Tonic function again. What makes the second phrase a consequent phrase, in other words a conclusive phrase, is the fact that the melody ends in the Tonic (F) and in the antecedent it ends in the third of the chord, giving us a feeling of continuation.

Now, let's add more diatonic chords to this progression in order to add more color and movement to the period. The melody will remain intact.

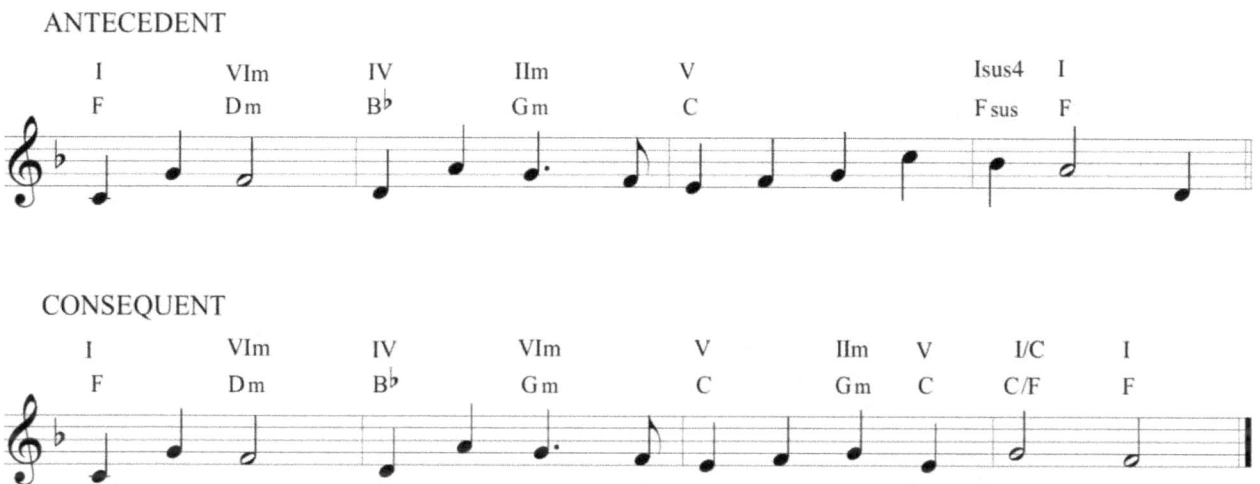

We can clearly hear an addition of color to this harmonic progression. This is a great way of adding more chords to a basic progression without changing the original function of the chord because the secondary diatonic chords belong to the same function as their preceding chords. (E.g.: In measure #1, F and Dm belong to the Tonic Function)

NOTE: Suspended chords (E.g.: Fsus on measure 4) are chords that contain the fourth degree instead of the third (in the case of Fsus, a Bb instead of an A). This provides a suspended sound that wants to resolve that fourth degree into the third of the chord (just like Fsus changes to F on measure 4)

# Applications of Contemporary Harmony I

## Cadences

*A cadence is a musical resolution that usually happens at the end of a phrase or at the end of a piece. It can be represented melodically, harmonically and/or rhythmically, and it provides a sense of conclusion.*

Melodic Cadences: When there is an intervallic movement that represents an ending or conclusion, such as: Ti – do, Sol – Do, etc. For example:

Basic Harmonic Cadences: When there is a chord or a combination of chords that is used to resolve to the Tonic or some other function or tonality. (We will discuss secondary dominants, modulation and more sophisticated cadences in a later chapter).

The basic harmonic cadences are as follow:

- Dominant to Tonic Cadence (The one used in most of the previous examples, usually at the end of a phrase or at the end of the piece):

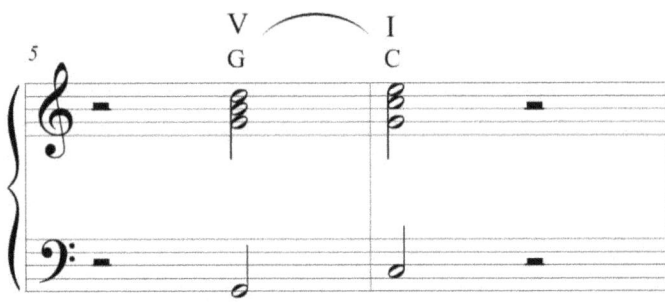

The arch pictured represents the movement of a descending 5th (Ascending 4th). This is one of many different symbols throughout the book that we will use continuously.

- **Tonic – Dominant – Tonic**: This is a very basic cadence with an emphasis on the Tonic chord since it's repeated before and after the Dominant.

In academic music, it is more common to use the Tonic in second inversion, in this case, with the bass in G, providing a Dominant pedal:

- **Sub-Dominant – Dominant to Tonic Cadence**: This is one of the most common cadences in tonal music because of its effectiveness. There is a harmonic movement around the three main diatonic functions. There are two common cadences for this category, the IV – V – I cadence and the II – V – I cadence. The first one is more common in classical music and the second one will become extremely common in Jazz and other popular styles of music. (We will talk more about this in Chapter 3)

IV – V – I Cadence:

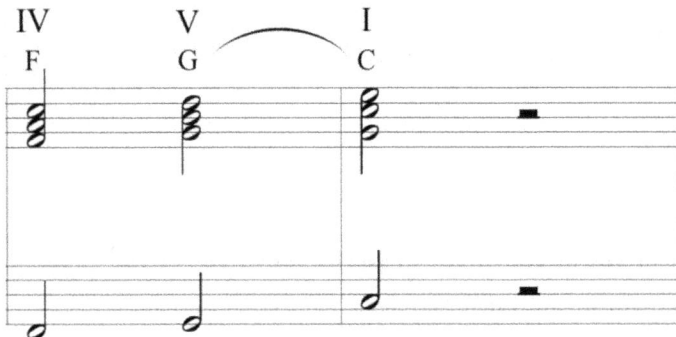

In this cadence, we go around the three principal chords from the functions. IV representing the Sub-Dominant, V representing the Dominant and I representing the Tonic.

## IIm – V – I Cadence:

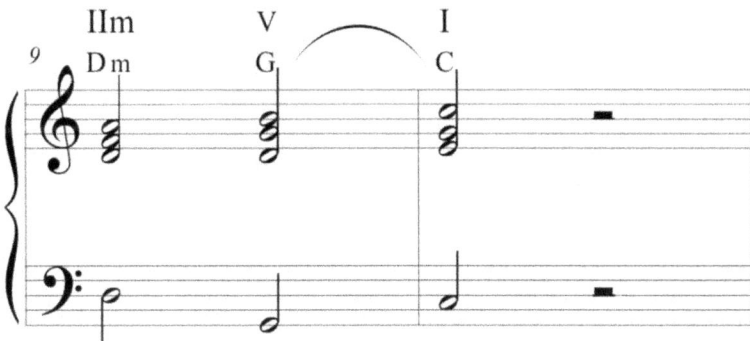

In this cadence, we replace the IV for IIm, which is the only secondary chord for the Sub-Dominant function; the rest remains the same as the previous example.

This cadence has a particular effectiveness because the bass is moving by descending fifths. D to G and G to C, providing a more conclusive sound.

- **Plagal Cadence**: This is basically a Sub-Dominant to Tonic cadence, which has a less conclusive sound since we don't have the Dominant function anymore. This cadence is still very effective, and is mainly used for a softer resolution. It is also known as the "Amen Cadence", since it is used a lot in church for that purpose.

## IV – I Cadence:

This cadence is also used with a tonic pedal, in this case C. This works great since that note also exists in the Sub-Dominant chord:

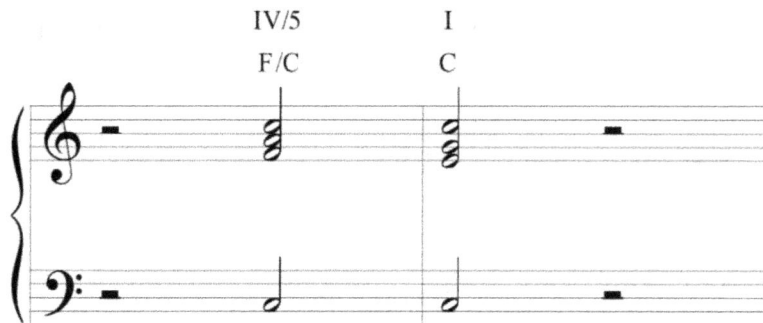

Let's see some examples of 4 bar melodic statements ending on cadences. Now we will combine melody, harmony and rhythm.

> NOTE: The following examples are in different keys. It is extremely important to understand all of these concepts in all 12 keys! For this reason, examples shown in this book will vary in key. This will help the student develop a functional understanding of harmony, allowing them to manipulate every key equally.

In these examples, we can see all of the harmonic cadences we've talked about so far used in a musical way at the end of every phrase. We can also see typical uses of diatonic harmony and how the 3 main functions work together in order to create a harmonic progression with a musical direction.

Let's see how all of these apply to an actual song.

This is *"Twinkle, Twinkle Little Star"* with its basic diatonic harmony and cadences:

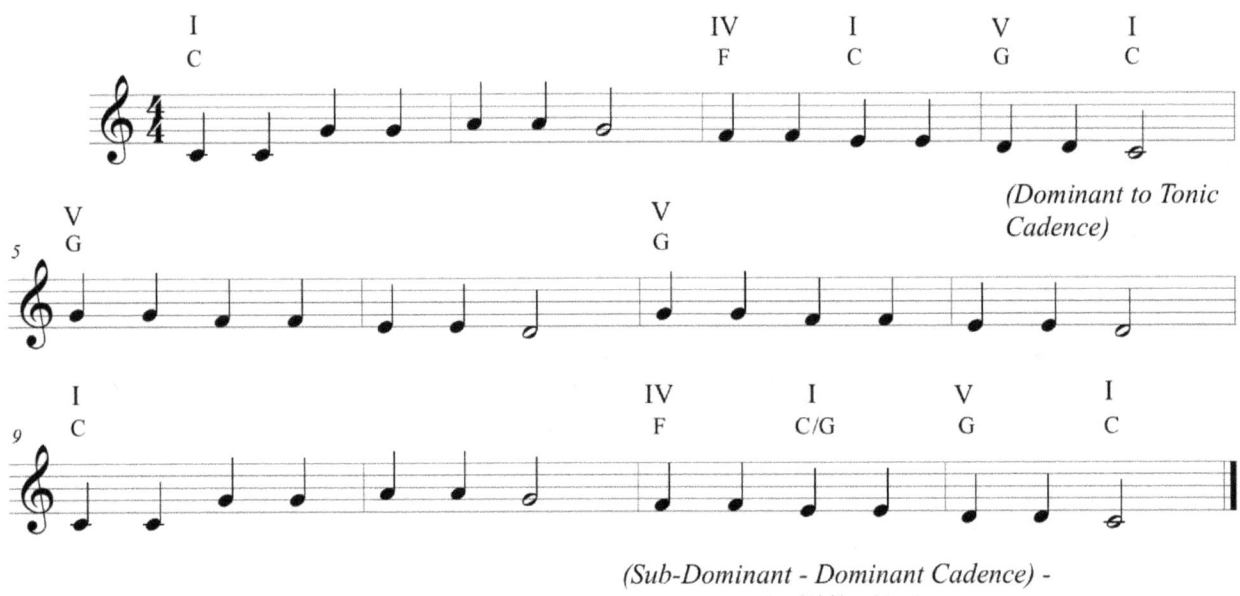

We can see how this song has an ABA melodic structure, each section lasting 4 measures. The first 4 measures (A) represent the equivalent of an *exposition*. The following 4 bars (B) represent a small *development* on the theme, and the last 4 bars (A) represent the *re-exposition* or *conclusion*. These names are used for classical music analysis but they also apply to many different forms on a lower scale, such as this song.

The song has a very simple harmonic progression and in this example we are only using primary diatonic chords. The exposition and conclusion are pretty much the same thing, with a small harmonic variation in the cadence at the end. The development stays in the Dominant chord providing tension thus, making the conclusion more effective as the tension is released when the chord resolves back to the Tonic.

Note that in the conclusion (last 4 measures) the Sub-Dominant – Dominant to Tonic cadence is emphasized even though we can see a tonic chord in the middle (C/G). This chord, when used in a cadence preceding the dominant chord, is usually acting as a suspension to the Dominant.

## Seventh Chords

A seventh chord is a triad with an extra major or minor third on top, depending on the harmonic situation. In diatonic harmony, we just add another diatonic third to each of the diatonic triads and this will give us a certain combination of intervals in between the chord tones, therefore giving us four options: Major seventh (Maj7) chords, *minor seventh* chords (m7), one *dominant seventh* chord (7) and one *minor seven flat 5* chord (m7(b5)) also known as *half-diminished* (ø). However, in this book we will use m7b5 exclusively.

Seventh chords are fuller and have more color than triads, since now we are dealing with a 4-note structure, rather than a 3-note structure.

Diatonic seventh chords don't change the function of the original triads; they just add more color to the same function.

This is how we convert a C triad into a C major seventh (Cmaj7):

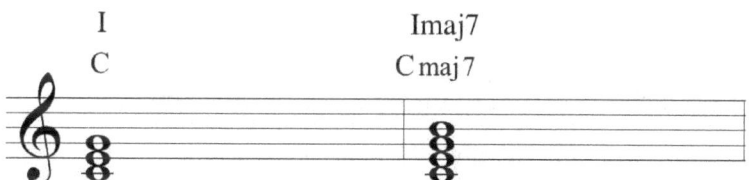

They both have the same function but the second one has more color added to it.

Seventh chords are spelled as follows:

-Major seventh chords: maj7 (E.g.: Cmaj7)
-Minor seventh chords: m7 or -7 (E.g.: Cm7 or C-7)
-Minor – Major seventh chords: mMaj7 (E.g.: CmMaj7)
-Dominant seventh chords: 7 (E.g.: C7)
-Half diminished chords or minor seventh flat 5: m7(b5) (E.g.: Cm7 (b5) )

- A major seventh chord is built out of a major third, a minor second and another major third:

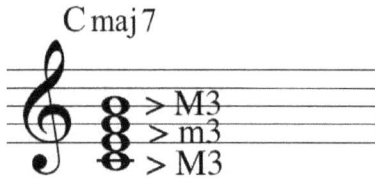

- A minor seventh chord is built out of a minor third, a major third and another minor third:

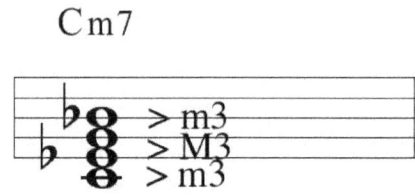

- A minor/major seventh chord is built out of a minor third and two major thirds:

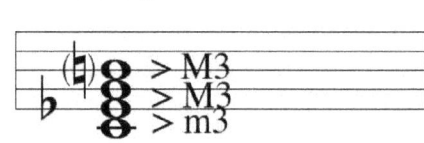

- A dominant seventh chord is built out of a major third and two minor thirds (This is an extremely important chord since it will be the core of resolutions and cadences, but we will talk about it later during this chapter):

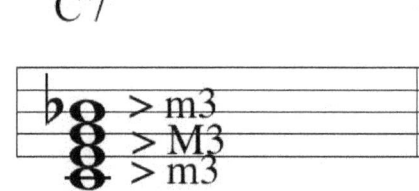

- A minor seventh flat 5 chord is built out of two minor thirds and one major third:

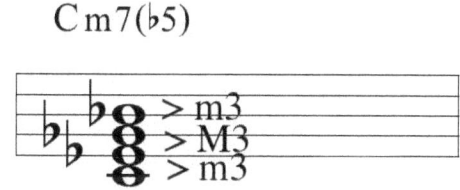

Now, let's see all the diatonic seventh chords in C major:

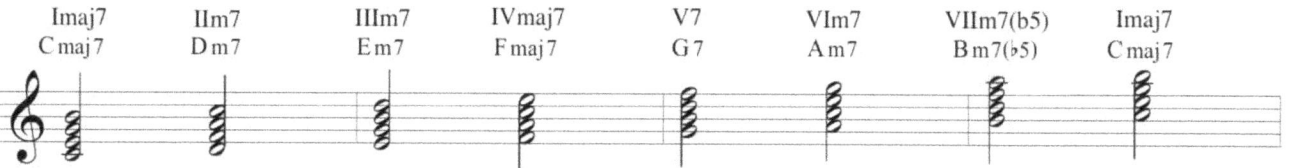

Our three diatonic functions are now going to be:

- Tonic Function: Imaj7 = Cmaj7, IIIm7 = Em7, VIm7 = Am7

- Sub-Dominant Function: IVmaj7 = Fmaj7, IIm7 = Dm7

- Dominant Function: V7 = G7

Now, we have a dominant seventh chord, which as we already know is made out of one major third and two minor thirds. The most important fact about these intervals is that now we get a *tri-tone interval* (augmented fourth or diminished fifth) between the third and the seventh of the chord, providing an even bigger tension than the regular dominant triad. This gives us a bigger expectation of resolution.

This tri-tone resolves by half steps; the third (B) will move up to the tonic (C), and the seventh of the chord (F) will move down to the third of the tonic chord (E):

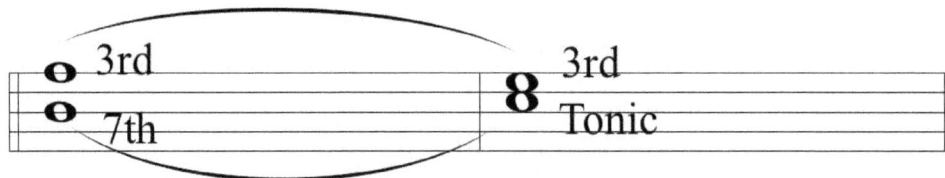

This is how it looks like functionally:

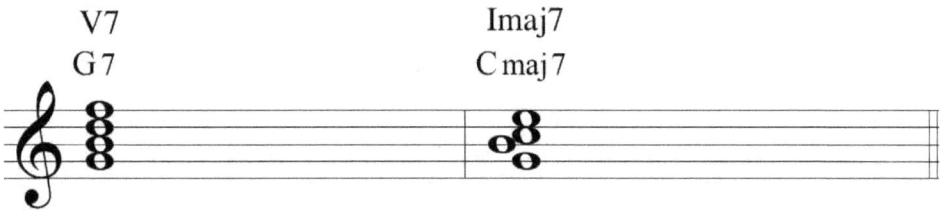

Now, we will be able to have stronger cadences with more color. Let's see some examples of small harmonic progressions using seventh chords:

A)

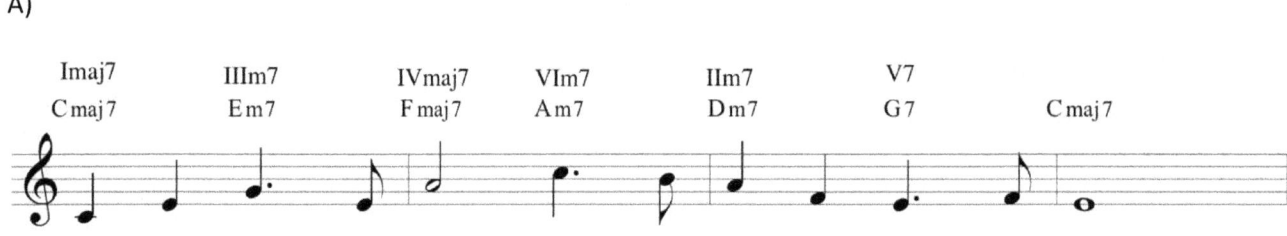

This is a similar example to one that we've seen before, but this time with seventh chords instead of triads, and with minor changes in the melody notes.

B)

Note how this harmonic progression doesn't start on the Tonic chord, it starts on the Sub-Dominant chord instead.

c)

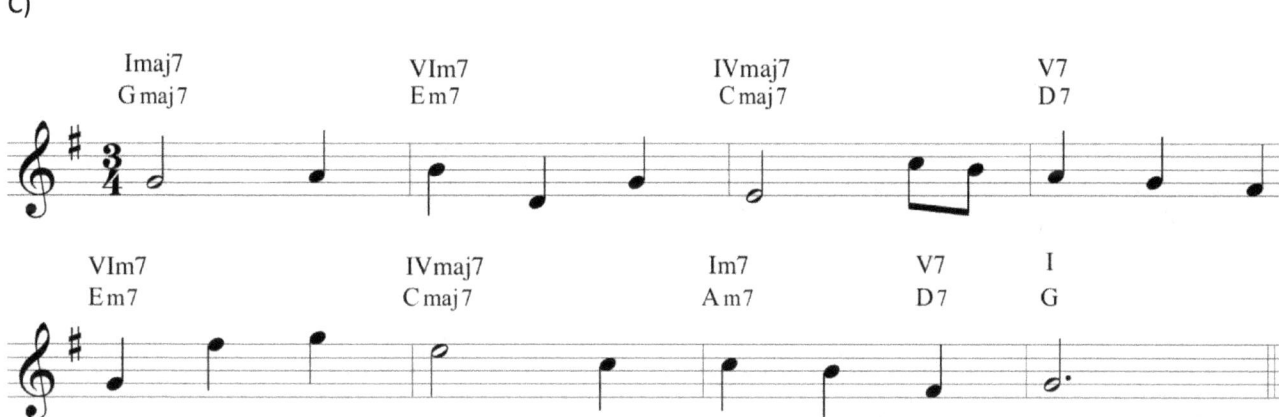

In this example we can see an 8 bar melody and harmonic progression in G major and in a 3/4 meter. Note how the last chord is a triad and not a seventh chord. This is because the melody lands on the tonic (G) and if the harmony would be Gmaj7 we would have a clash between the notes F# and G. Also note how the D7 chord on measure 7 is placed on the third beat, which is the most common placement of a second chord within the same measure on a ¾ time signature.

NOTE: Don't forget to study all the diatonic seventh chords in every key!

22 | *Applications of Contemporary Harmony I*

These are the diatonic seventh chords in some keys that are closely related to C major in the circle of fifths:

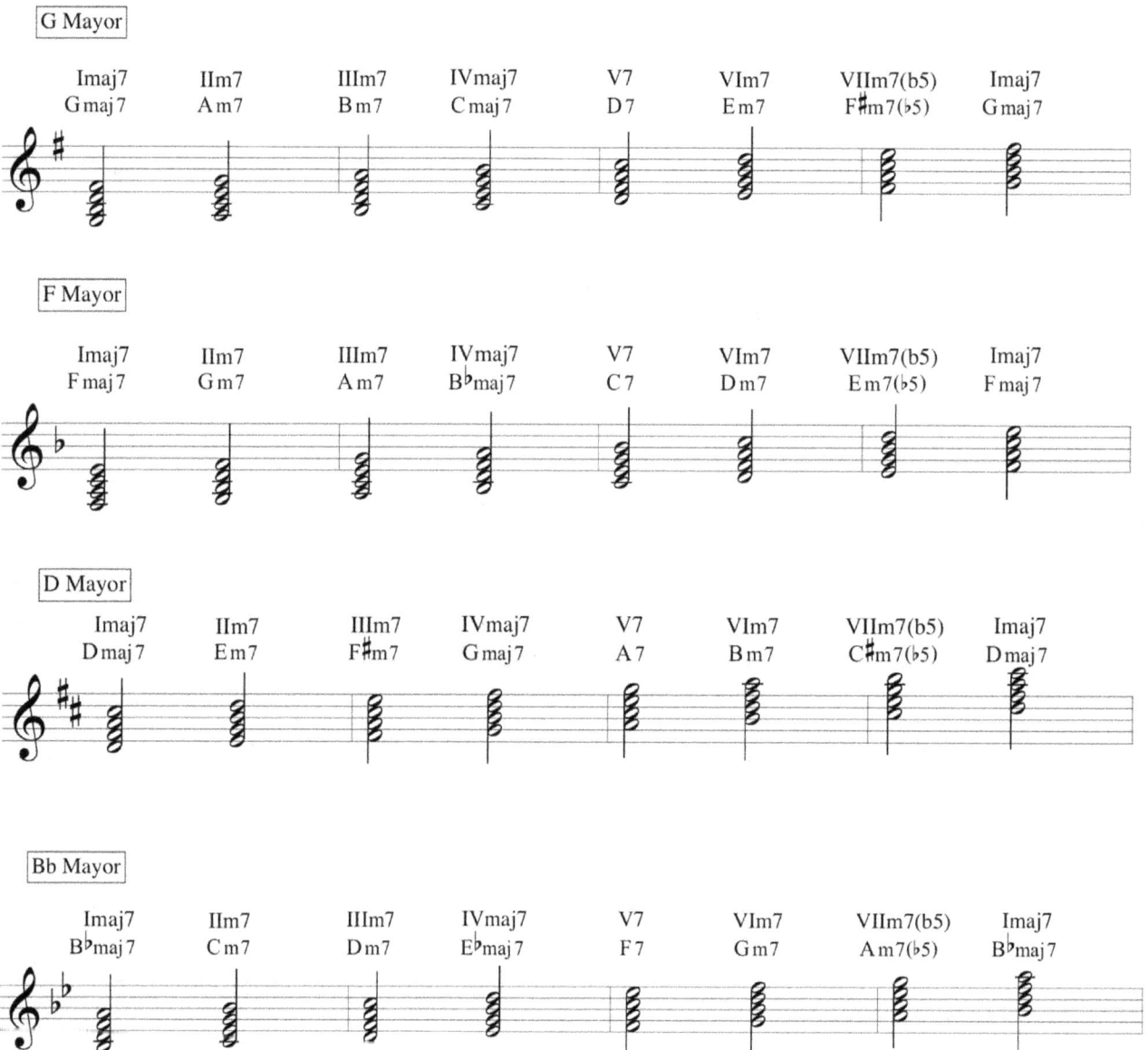

## Inversions

An *inversion* is the position of any given chord; this is to say how the chord will be executed or, better said, "voiced" (Directly related to the subject of voicings, which we will talk about extensively on *"Applications of Contemporary Harmony II"*). The inversion of a chord can drastically change the intention of the harmony, even though the function remains the same.

There are three inversions that exist:

ROOT POSITION (Original): This is the natural position of a chord with the root in the bass.

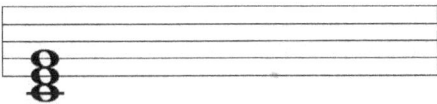

1. First Inversion: This is when the third of the chord is in the bass, in the case of a C triad, it would be the note E:

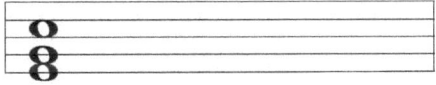

2. Second Inversion: This is when the fifth of the chord is in the bottom.

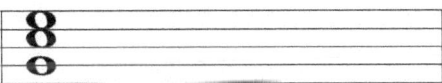

24 | *Applications of Contemporary Harmony I*

Now let's look at the same inversions (plus the third one) with a seventh chord:

1. ROOT POSITION (With seventh)

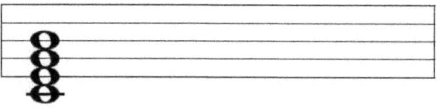

2. Second Inversion (With seventh):

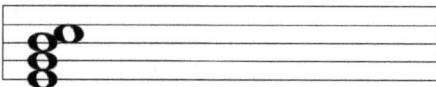

3. Third Inversion (IT ONLY EXISTS WITHIN A SEVENTH CHORD): This is when the seventh is at the bottom.

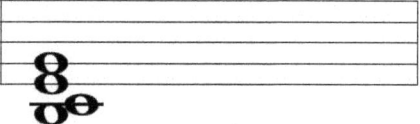

## Basic Voice Leading

*Voice leading* can be understood as the efficient movement of the voices and/or most practical.

This is basically how to connect one chord with the next efficiently in a given harmonic progression. Jazz pianist do it all the time while comping* over a harmonic progression on a Jazz standard and you can also you hear it constantly in Bach´s fugues. Not only is it extremely important how you voice a chord, but also how you connect it to the following chord. In order to voice lead properly, you must understand inversions profoundly, since they are crucial when deciding a voicing pattern.

*Comping: A Jazz term that refers to the harmonic accompaniment usually provided by the pianist or guitarist.*

There are certain guidelines to follow while attempting to do a good voice leading.

1. Keep any common tone between the two chords: This will guarantee efficiency and will give us the best sounding result, since it will avoid a drastic movement from one chord and the other.

2. Move the remaining tones by step to the nearest chord tone: This will provide economical movement either upwards or downwards, depending on availability, convenience and/or purpose.

For example:

This is a C major triad followed by an F major triad with no voice leading at all (Both chords in root position):

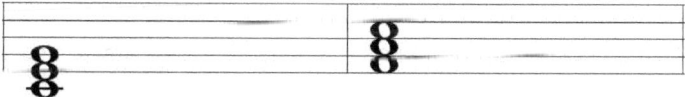

Now, these are the two same chords with an efficient voice leading:

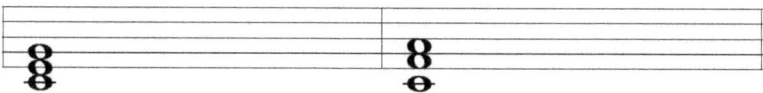

## 26 | *Applications of Contemporary Harmony I*

Notice how the C stays static since it's the note that both chords share in common. The two remaining notes move by step, in this case upwards. As a result, we end up with an F major chord in second inversion (with the fifth at the bottom).

Now, let's start on a different inversion to see where the voice leading takes us:

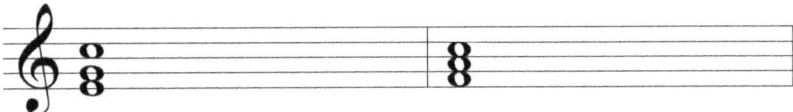

Notice how when we start our progression with a C major chord in first inversion, the closest way to go to F major will be F in Root position. Again, the note C remains static since it's the common tone between the two chords, and the remaining notes move by step.

This is how it looks like if we start in second inversion:

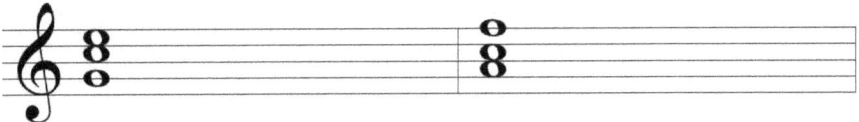

Here is the same principle applied to a I – V progression:

In this case the common tone between the two chords is G, so we keep it intact. The remaining two notes move by step, in this case downwards.

Let's see how a basic voice leading would work for a I – IV – V – I harmonic progression in C major, starting in root position:

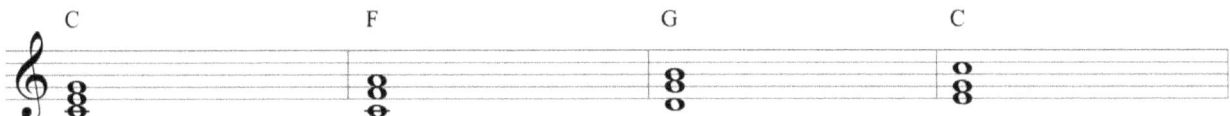

From I to IV (C to F) we keep the C as a common tone and move the remaining two notes one step up. Between IV and V (F and G) there are no common tones, therefore all notes have to move a step, in this case going up. Finally, from V to I (G to C) we have G as a common tone, so we keep that note and move the remaining two by step, in this case going up.

Using these techniques the student will be able to efficiently connect any possible progression, as odd as some of them may seem. Voice leading is what holds a harmonic progression together; it makes it have sense. Without it, we only have separate functions moving by large intervals and lacking connection. We will explore this subject further on *"Applications of Contemporary Harmony II"*.

Voice leading works exactly the same with seventh chords, the only additional factor is that now we will have to deal with third inversions. Let's look at the same I – IV – V – I harmonic progression with seventh chords, starting on root position.

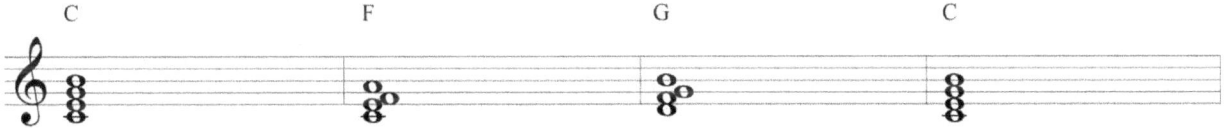

Let's analyze the voice leading of this example:

- Between I and IV (C and F): We have 2 common tones that we keep, C and G. The B moves down to A and G moves down to F.

- Between IV and V (F and G): No common tones. All notes move up by step.

- Between V and I (G and C): Two Common Tones that we keep, B and G. The F moves down to E and D moves down to C.

## Modes formed out of major scale degrees

*Modes* are alternate scales that result from building a diatonic major or minor scale using as a reference another diatonic degree, different than the tonic.

The major scale that we've been studying so far is actually a mode, known as the *Ionian mode*. There are seven modes within a major scale constructed by every single pitch in the scale. The way to figure out these modes is to write the major scale starting from every note of the scale.

This will give us the 7 most important modes: *Ionian, Dorian, Phrygian, Lydian, Mixolydian, Aeolian* (Natural Minor), and *Locrian*.

Each of these scales will not only have a melodic representation but also a harmonic one since they will be the scale representing each of the diatonic chords. E.g.: Cmaj7 will be represented by the C IONIAN mode. (This is a topic called chord scales, which will be mentioned later in this book)

Let's take a look at all the modes related to C major with the respective diatonic chords that they are representing:

As you can see, each of the scale degrees are represented in relationship to their chord or root. Please keep in mind that all the 2nd, 4th and 6th degrees are also named 9th, 11th and 13th. This is related to chord scale theory and tensions, which will be a subject discussed thoroughly in Chapter 5. For now, let's refer to them as 2nd, 4th and 6th degrees only.

## Non-Chord tones

Just like the name expresses, *non-chord tones* are those notes that don't belong to the chordal structure. These are usually notes from the chord scale (mode belonging to the chord) that are acting as a passing tone, neighbor tone, etc. They are usually placed in between chord tones and on a weak beat.

There are five main types of non-chord tones:

NOTE: Every example shows the melodic degree of the respective chords.

***Passing tones (PT):*** *Notes that are placed in between two different chord tones, usually in a weak beat.*

***Neighbor tones (NT):*** *Notes that are placed in between the same note.*

***Escape tones (ET):*** *Notes that are placed after a leap from a chord tone. An escape note has to resolve to a chord tone after it happens.*

**Suspension (Sus):** *These are basically passing tones that are placed in a strong beat, as opposed to a weak beat, and they **always** go down to a chord tone.*

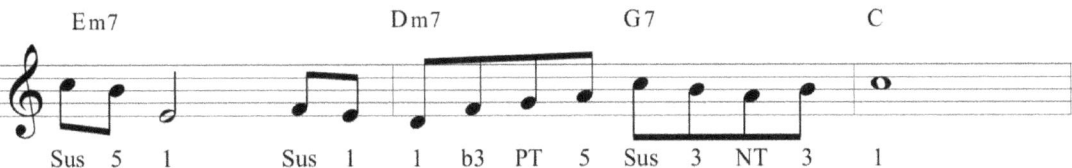

**Retardation (Ret):** *These are just like suspensions, but they resolve **up** instead of down and they always happen on a strong beat (as opposed to chromatic passing tones or neighbor tones, which usually happen on a weak beat):*

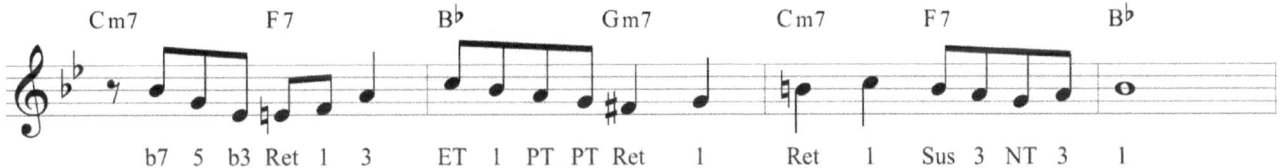

Note that this example also demonstrates the use of other non-chord tones.

**Appoggiatura (AP):** *Is a non-chord tone that has no preceding note but it is always followed with a chord tone (It can also come after an Escape Tone).*

NOTE: You will see more examples of these in the next and last section of this chapter.

## 32 | Applications of Contemporary Harmony I

Let's take a look at how all the non-chord tones work together:

PASSING TONES (PT) AND SUSPENSIONS (SUS):

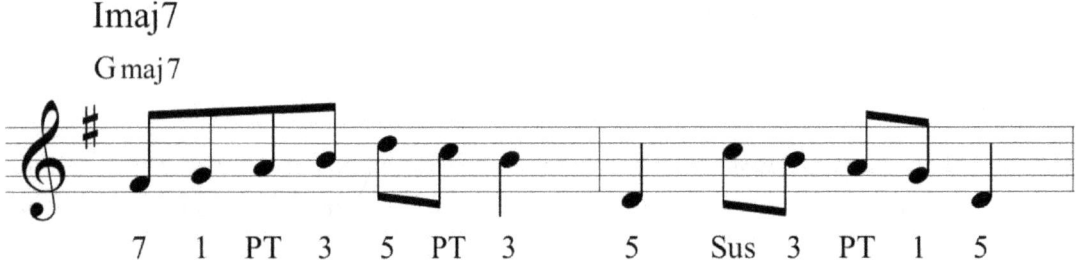

PASSING TONES (PT), SUSPENSIONS (SUS), ESCAPE TONES (ET) AND NEIGHBOR TONES (NT)

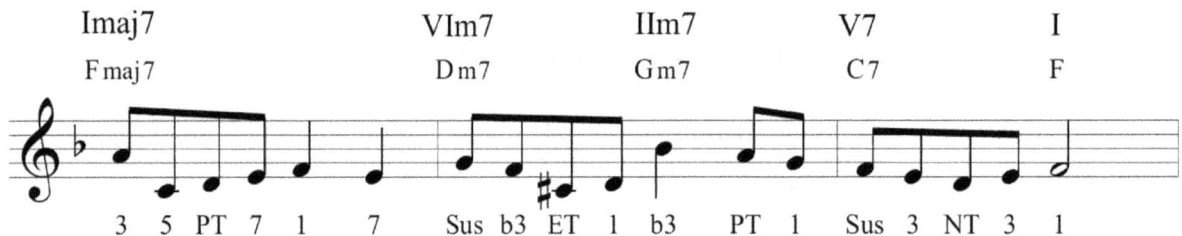

PASSING TONES (PT), NEIGHBOR TONES (NT) AND ESCAPE TONES (ET)

(This example contains a chord from a topic that we have not yet covered – B7)

PASSING TONES (PT), NEIGHBOR TONE (NT), ESCAPE TONES (ET), SUSPENSIONS (SUS), RETARDATIONS (RET) AND APPOGGIATURAS (AP):

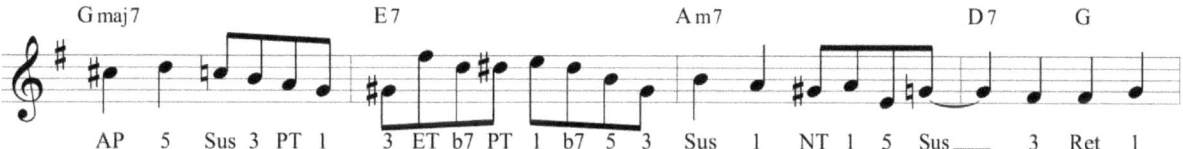

Note that in some of the later examples, some chromatic non-chord tones have been placed. These work exactly the same as the regular non-chord tones, but provide a much colorful effect since they are usually non-diatonic.

We will spell the chromatic non-chord tones as CPT (chromatic passing tone), CNT (chromatic neighbor tone) and CAP (chromatic appoggiatura).

# Application: Combining diatonic melodies with diatonic harmonies

These are a series of examples in which you will see how diatonic melodies work together with diatonic harmonies with all of the topics that we have covered so far.

This includes diatonic major harmony, antecedent-consequent phrases, seventh chords and non-chord tones (including chromatic non-chord tones).

All of the examples will be displayed in a "lead sheet" form, which basically means melody with chord symbols. No written chords and inversions will be displayed.

1.

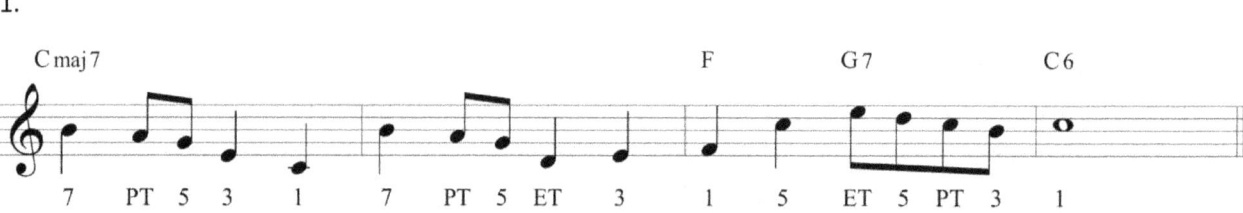

In this example we can clearly see the use of a Sub-Dominant – Dominant to Tonic cadence (IV – V7 – I) at the end. This is also a good example of diatonic passing tones and escape tones. The last chord is a C6, which is just the triad with an added sixth, in this case the note A.

2.

In this example we can also see a Sub-Dominant – Dominant to Tonic cadence (IIm7- - V7 – I). This is a good example of diatonic and chromatic neighbor tones (CNT). Note that in the first measure we have two neighbor tones, one on top of the target note (B) and the other one below; this is called a double neighbor tone.

3.

This is a good example of a musical Period composed by an antecedent phrase and a consequent phrase, both being almost the same until the last cadence. The antecedent phrase ends on the dominant chord, providing an inconclusive sonority and the consequent phrase ends on a Dominant to Tonic cadence, providing resolution and therefore a conclusion.

Melodically, we can see the use of chromatic neighbor tones and escape tones (measure 1 and 2), this will take us away a little bit from the diatonic sound.

4.

Another Period. Both phrases are almost identical until the respective cadences; the antecedent ends on a Sub-Dominant to Dominant cadence with no resolution to the tonic until the consequent phrase, which finally ends on a Sub-Dominant – Dominant to Tonic cadence providing conclusion.

5.

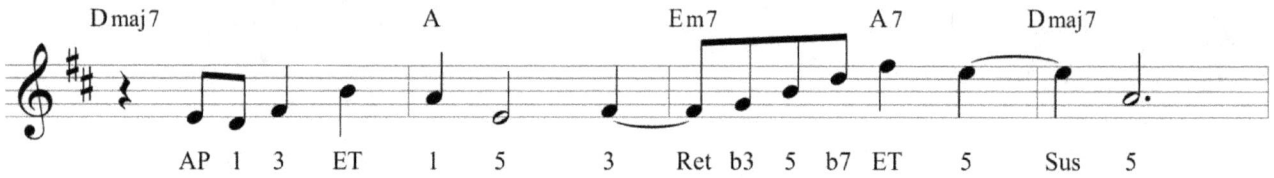

This is a good example of an appoggiatura (E to D).

6.

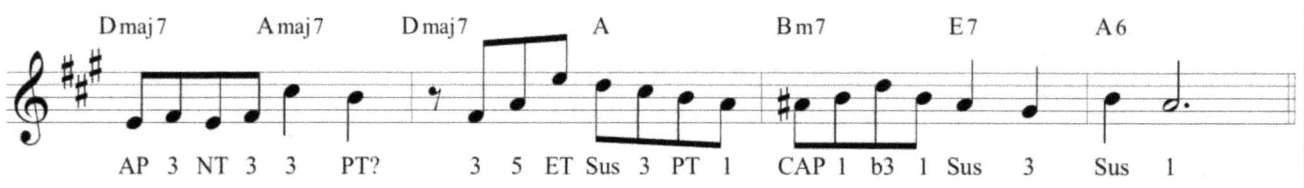

# [2]

# Harmonization 1 - Using only Diatonic Harmony

HARMONIZATION is the art of providing a certain color to a given melody. It is one of the fundamentals of music composition and it is of great importance because every single decision that you make can completely change the character of the melody. In this chapter we will only discuss the application of diatonic harmony, and how to use it effectively in order to provide the desired color to a melody.

# 38 | Applications of Contemporary Harmony I

Let's take a simple diatonic melody as an example:

The first thing that we have to do when presented with a diatonic melody like this is to look at the form of the piece, melodic fragment, etc. Remember that functional harmony exists because of form, so that is always the first thing to consider. In this case we can see that there is a *"call and response"* between the first 4 measures and the following 4. This is just like a musical period, but with a much different consequent than what we would usually have, since the melody of the first 4 measures is not being repeated exactly. So let's divide the two sections into phrase A and phrase B; phrase A acts as an antecedent, and phrase B acts as a consequent.

Now that we've divided the song into two sections, we try to look for all the melodic cadences; this basically means when the melody is implying a dominant to tonic resolution. If we use a musical period as an example, we know that there is usually a cadence at the end of each section; in this case our sections are phrase A and phrase B. Therefore, we can assume that the whole piece will end with a dominant to tonic cadence (Measure 7 would have a G chord, and measure 8 a C chord), and the same thing will happen for measure 3 and 4, since the melody is implying the same thing.

Notice that I didn't start harmonizing from the first bar. Once the form of the piece is clear and the melodic cadences have been identified, you can start harmonizing the cadences first; this way you will have a much clearer sense of direction and you will be able to better accommodate the preceding chords.

This is how it looks like so far:

Both phrases end with a Dominant to Tonic cadence. Note that in measure 7 (1 measure before the end) we get a C chord in second inversion because the E in the melody is not part of a G chord, then we change to a G chord and finally resolve to C. This particular chord acts as a harmonic suspension when followed by the dominant chord, so both chords have a dominant function. Also note that in measure 3 we have a melody note A over a G chord; this note is acting as a long neighbor tone in between the melody note G from the previous measure and the other G from measure 3.

Let's continue our harmonization by going back from our cadences all the way to the beginning of each phrase. We will start with phrase A. If we take a look at the notes in measure 2, they pretty much imply a G chord since we have the notes B and G, so we extend the G chord through measures 2 and 3. Now we are left with the first measure, which will tend to be the tonic *chord (NOTE: don't generalize the idea that every piece of music has to start with the tonic chord since it is not true)*. In this case, since we have a G chord on measure 2, we probably want to get there either from the tonic chord (C) or from the sub-dominant chord (F). The sub-dominant chord could fit the first half of the measure since we have the note A, and the tonic chord could fit perfectly for the second half of the measure since we have the melody notes G and C. The problem with starting the phrase with the sub-dominant chord is that it will not sound as natural and it will define the first measure with a sub-dominant function, which could be done, but it is not the best option for the beginning of this song. The chord that would fit best is a C6 chord (the tonic chord with an added 6$^{th}$).

40 | *Applications of Contemporary Harmony I*

Now let's finish harmonizing the second phrase. Again, if we work our way back from our cadence we will have a much clearer idea of what chord will fit best in order to create a more effective chord progression. If we work our way back from measure 7, where we have the C chord in second inversion and the dominant to tonic cadence, we see that the notes on the second half of measure 6 (melody notes A and F) are implying a sub-dominant sound (F chord or Dm chord), so now we have to decide which one of the two will fit better.

Take a look at the first half of that measure, you will see the melody note B held for two beats. We know that note usually represents a G chord or another form of the dominant function, but in this case it is acting as a long passing tone between melody notes C (from the previous measure) and A (right after the B), so it is probably a better choice to harmonize the entire measure with an F chord. (The note B will not sound very effective over a Dm chord; we will discuss this later in this book).

At this point we only have one measure left to harmonize (measure 5). This situation is a lot easier than before, because now we know the preceding chord and the following chord; we basically know where we are coming from and where we are going. Another thing to note is that measure 5 is the beginning of phrase B, so we probably want to harmonize it with the tonic function again.

## Basic Diatonic Reharmonization

*Reharmonization* is the art of changing the color of a given melody. Now that we know how to harmonize a simple diatonic melody, we will learn how to reharmonize a diatonic melody that already has a predetermined harmony. In this chapter, we will only learn how to re-harmonize with diatonic harmony.

We will use the same example as before.

This is the happy birthday song with the harmonic progression that we've already predetermined:

The easiest way to start reharmonizing with alternate diatonic chords is to analyze the functions of the chords in the original harmonic progression, and then start using the alternate chords from that function. If we are in C major (like in the happy birthday example) and the chord in measure 4 is C, we know it belongs to the tonic function; so we could potentially replace that chord with another chord from the tonic function, in this case an Em (IIIm) or an Am (VIm). In order to do this, we have to make sure that the melody notes can fit properly with the new chord, either as a chord tone or as a non-chord tone.

Let's break down our diatonic reharmonization measure by measure:

Abbreviations used:   T.F= Tonic Function
S-D.F= Sub-dominant Function
D.F= Dominant Function

| Measure # | Original Chord and Function | Possible Alternate Chord(s) from the same Function |
|---|---|---|
| 1 | C6 (T.F) | Em , Am (T. F) |
| 2 | G (D.F) | Bm7(b5) (D.F) |
| 3 | G (D.F) | Bm7(b5) (D.F) |
| 4 | C (T.F) | Em , Am (T.F) |
| 5 | C (T.F) | Em , Am (T.F) |
| 6 | F (S-D.F) | Dm (S-D.F) |
| 7 | C/G, G (D.F) | Bm7(b5) (D.T) |
| 8 | C (T.F) | Em, Am (T.F) |

Now we've determined all the alternate diatonic chords that could easily replace the chords in the original harmonic progression because they belong to the same diatonic function.

Let's see how a reharmonized version of the happy birthday song would look like. For this example, I'm replacing some of the original chords with some of the alternate chords from the third column of the table.

*NOTE: You don't have to reharmonize every single chord. The art of reharmonization is based on replacing and/or adding chords when you feel they will provide an effective change of color to the melody, not just to overwhelm the harmonic progression with too many chords.*

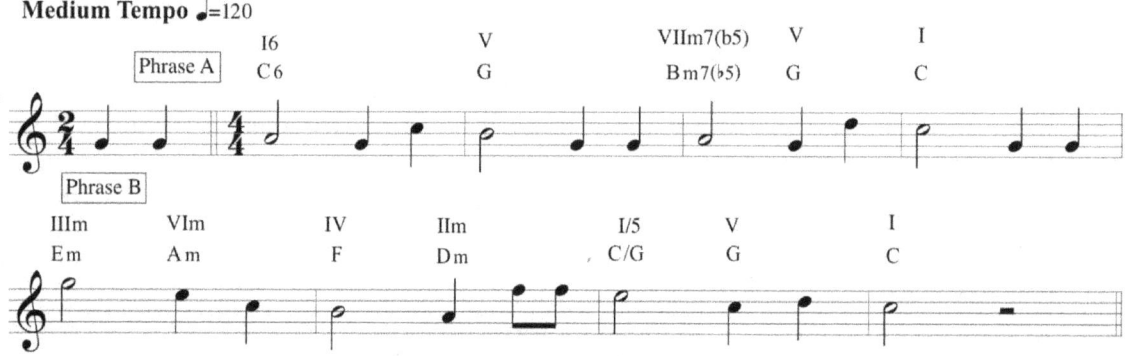

Notice that I've only reharmonized measures 3, 5 and 6.

In measure 3, I added the VIIm7(5) chord from the dominant function to generate more movement. On measure 5, I replaced the C chord for and Em chord and I added an Am chord after that for more movement. The same happens on measure 6 with the added Dm chord from the Sub-Dominant function.

Note that in many situations, reharmonization can consist on adding additional chords either from the same function or from other functions, just like I did on the previous example. This will increase the harmonic beat of the passage (This is a good tool to use if there is only one chord per measure in the original harmonic progression).

Let's take a look at the same thing but this time with a functional explanation:

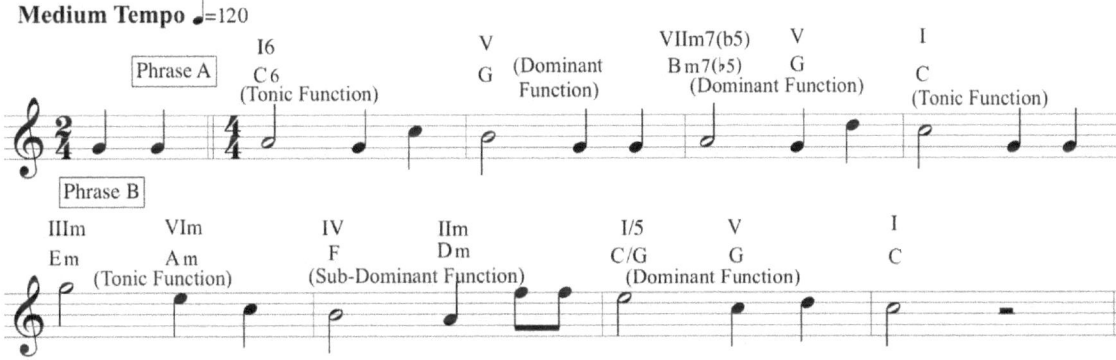

Let's go through the same process of harmonizing and then reharmonizing with this new 8 bar diatonic melody in G major.

## 44 | *Applications of Contemporary Harmony I*

Just like we did before, we first try to identify the form of the piece and then figure out the cadences at the end of every phrase. This melody has the same form as the happy birthday song, it is an 8 bar melody divided into two 4 bar phrases: Phrase A and Phrase B.

Since it's a diatonic melody, it is very likely that it will end on the tonic chord in order to conclude the piece of music; therefore it will have some kind of cadence at the end. If we analyze the melody notes of measure 7 (one measure before the end) we see that we can easily fit a D chord (Dominant) and resolve to a G chord (Tonic) in the last measure. We can also agree that the last measure of phrase A (measure 4) implies a dominant chord because of the F# in the melody, so we can go ahead and harmonize the whole measure with a D chord.

This is how it looks like up to this point:

Now we can continue harmonizing Phrase A by working our way back from the D chord on measure 4. If we take a look at the notes on measure 3, we can see that there is a clear implication of a G chord because of the emphasis on the melody note B (The third of the chord). In this measure the melody note A is acting as a passing tone between the B and the G and the melody note C is acting both as an escape tone (coming from the note G) and as a suspension to the note B.

Measure 2 could be a G6 chord (because of the E in the melody) or it could easily be a sub-dominant chord (C or Am). The latter option would be more effective since we will most likely harmonize measure 1 with the tonic chord, so it is better to change to a sub-dominant function on measure 2.

This is how Phrase A would look like:

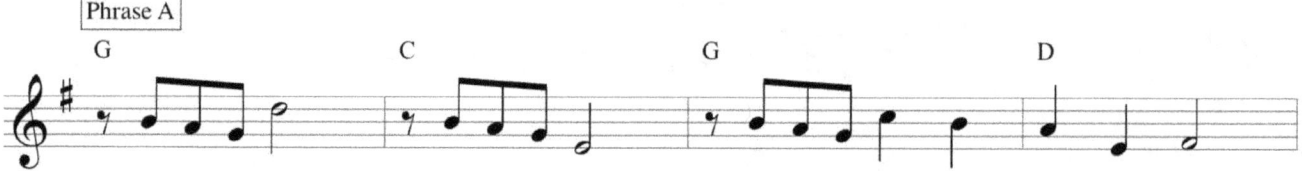

These is the functional analysis:

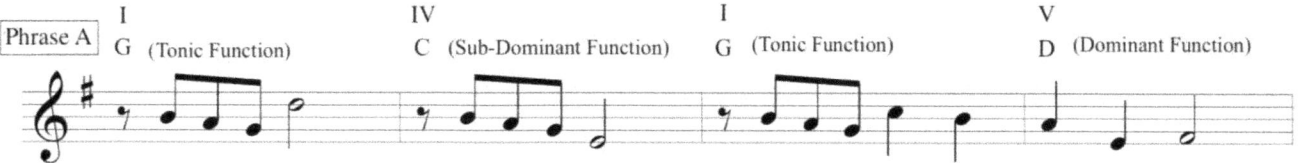

This is a great example of simple diatonic harmonization using the three main functions (Tonic, Sub-Dominant and Dominant)

Now let's proceed with harmonizing Phrase B (measure 5 and 6).

The melody notes on measure 5 imply either an Em chord or a Cmaj7 chord. Since we are not using 7th chords to harmonize yet, let's use the Em chord, which is a secondary chord from the tonic function (VIm). Measure 6 also implies an Em chord or a C chord; let's use the C chord for variation and also to change the function in order to provide the melody with more harmonic movement.

This is how measure 5 and 6 would look like:

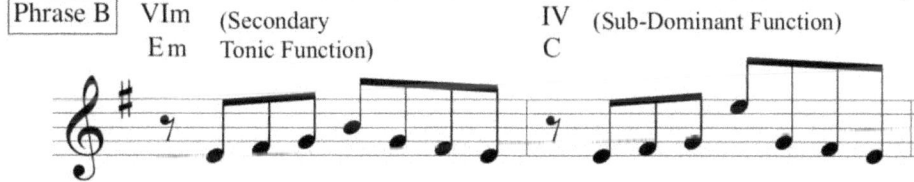

Now that we have finished harmonizing this 8 bar melody, let's see how it looks like with a complete harmonic and melodic analysis:

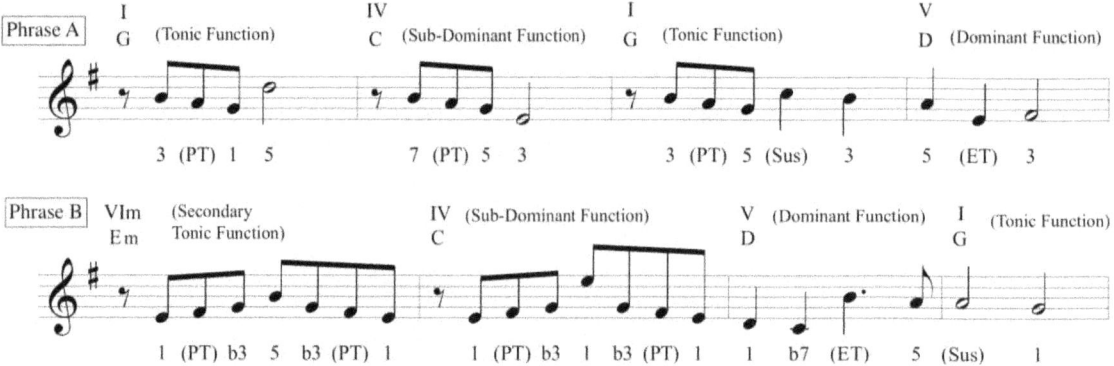

NOTE: All the melodic analysis is based on the section *"non-chord tones"* from chapter 1.

Now that we have settled a basic diatonic harmonic progression for this melody, we can start reharmonizing.

Just like we did with the happy birthday song, one of the easiest ways to provide a harmonic variation is to replace some of the chords with alternate chords that belong to the same function. Before doing this, we have to always analyze the melody notes in relation to the new chord to see if they will work well together.

In the following table, you can see all the possible alternate diatonic chords that have the same function as the original chord used on each measure of the previous melody:

Abbreviations:

- T.F = Tonic Function
- S-D.F = Sub-Dominant Function
- D.F = Dominant Function
- Sec T.F = Secondary Tonic Function chord
- Sec S-D.F = Secondary Sub-Dominant function chord
- Sec D.F = Secondary Dominant Function chord

| Measure # | Original Chord and Function | Possible Alternate Chord/s from the same Function |
|---|---|---|
| 1 | G (T.F) | Em, Bm (T.F) |
| 2 | C (S-D.F) | Am (S-D.F) |
| 3 | G (T.F) | Em, Bm (T.F) |
| 4 | D (D.F) | F#m7(b5) (D.F) |
| 5 | Em (Sec. T.F) | Gmaj, Bm (T.F) |
| 6 | C (S-D.F) | Am (S-D.F) |
| 7 | D (D.F) | F#m7(b5) (D.F) |
| 8 | G (T.F) | Em, Bm (T.F) |

You should not feel restricted to reharmonize the measure only with a chord from the same function; this is just an easy way to start. You can decide to change the function on a given measure or even split the measure into two different functions (Especially for a cadence). You will see this in the following reharmonizations:

# 48 | *Applications of Contemporary Harmony I*

## Diatonic Reharmonization 1:

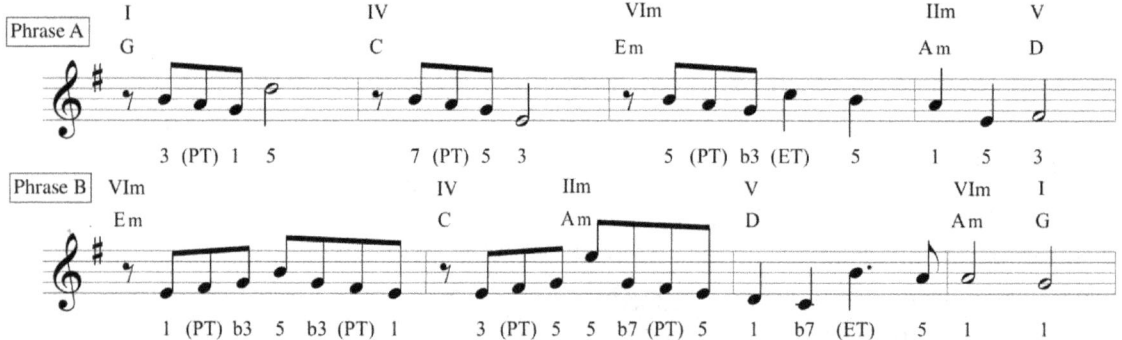

In this example you can see how in measure 3, we replaced the G chord for an Em chord, which is a secondary chord from the tonic function. Measure 2 is a good example of re-harmonizing by splitting the measure into two different functions; we've added an Am chord (secondary sub-dominant chord) in the first half of the measure, and we kept the D chord (primary dominant function) from the original progression in the second half of the measure. Measure 6 is a good example of adding a chord from the same function as in the original harmonic progression in order to provide more movement to the progression; we see that the Am (secondary sub-dominant chord) has been added to the second half of the measure. Finally, we can see the addition of an Am chord in the last measure; this will change the character of the melody note since now it won't be a non-chord tone as before, this time it will be a chord tone.

Notice how the melody notes below the new chords change their melodic function/ scale degree.

## Diatonic reharmonization 2:

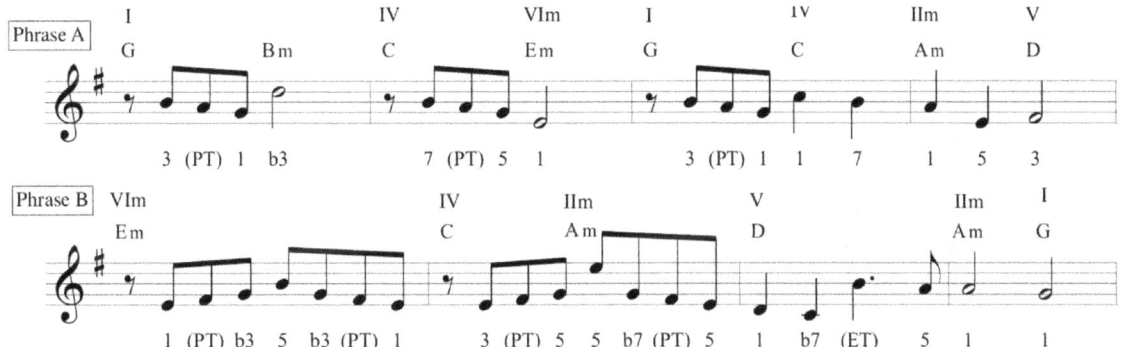

Let's do an explanation measure by measure.

Remember the abbreviations:
- T.F = Tonic Function
- S-D.F = Sub-Dominant Function
- D.F = Dominant Function
- Sec T.F = Secondary Tonic Function chord
- Sec S-D.F = Secondary Sub-Dominant function chord
- Sec D.F = Secondary Dominant Function chord

| Measure # | Original chord (from original chord progression) | Reharmonization: Alternate chord/added chords |
|---|---|---|
| 1 | G (T.F) | G (T.F) and Bm (Sec T.F) |
| 2 | C (S-D.F) | C (S-D.F) and Em (Sec T.F) |
| 3 | G (T.F) | G (T.F) and C (S-D.F) |
| 4 | D (D.F) | Am (Sec S-D.F) and D (D.F) |
| 5 | Em (Sec T.F) | Em (Sec T.F) |
| 6 | C (S-D.F) | C (S-D.F) and Am (Sec S-D.F) |
| 7 | D (D.F) | D (D.F) |
| 8 | G (T.F) | Am (Sec S-D.F) and G (T.F) |

# Reharmonizing with Diatonic Seventh Chords

Reharmonizing with diatonic seventh chords works in the same manner as with regular triads (the way we've been doing it so far), but this time we have one additional available chord tone to consider: the 7$^{th}$. By using 7$^{th}$ chords to harmonize you will be able to provide a richer color to a given melody.

We can basically have the exact same reharmonization as in the previous example, but this time adding the corresponding diatonic 7$^{th}$ to each chord.

This is how it would look like:

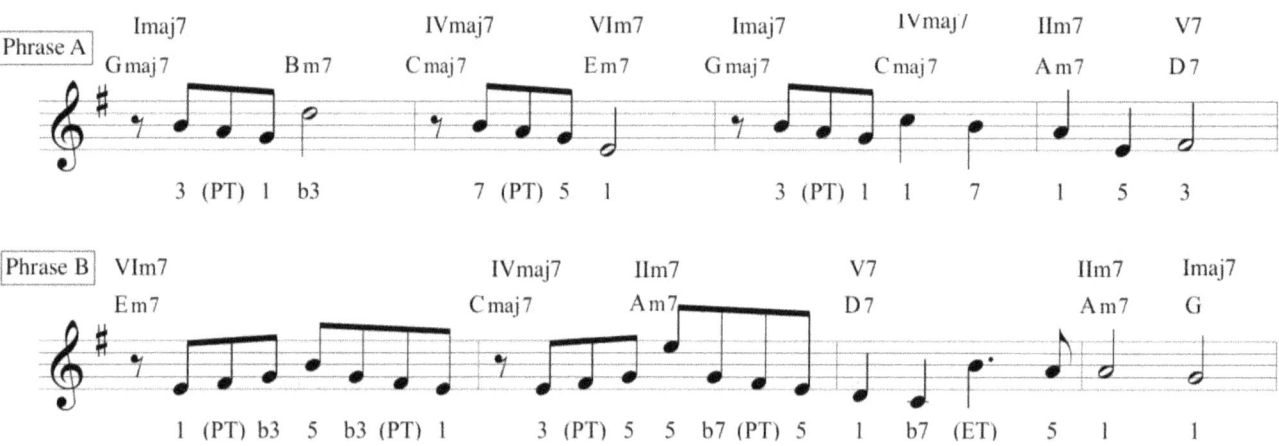

This reharmonization will sound fuller and slightly more complex than the previous examples because of the 7$^{th}$ chords.

Note that in some cases the melody note is actually the 7$^{th}$:

- Measure 2: Melody note B over a Cmaj7 chord
- Measure 3: Melody note B over a Cmaj7 chord
- Measure 6: Melody note G over an Am7 chord
- Measure 7: Melody note C over a D7 chord

For the next example, we will see how we can use the 7th of the diatonic chords as an important melody note (In the last example we identified some sevenths as melody notes, but they were clearly not the most important notes because of their duration, as well as the fact that most of them where placed on an upbeat*.)

NOTE: It is important to know that the Non-chord tones are usually placed on a weak beat* or upbeat* (except for suspensions and retardations). The downbeats* are better suited for chord tones in order to avoid dissonance.

*Downbeat: It's the term given to the beats of a measure (E.g.: In a 4/4 meter, the downbeats will be 1, 2, 3 and 4.

*Weak Beat: It happens on the secondary beats of a given measure. In a 4/4-meter, we say that beats 1 and 3 are strong and beats 2 and 4 are weak.

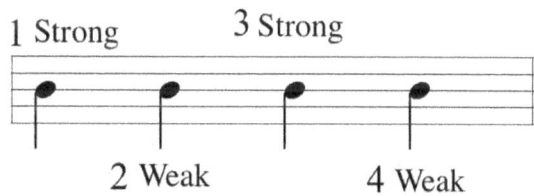

*Upbeat: This term is used for the smaller subdivisions inside a measure (eighth notes or less). An upbeat is what happens in between the downbeats of a measure (E.g.: In Measure #2 of the previous image, we can see the melody note B being placed after an eighth note rest; hence this note is placed on an upbeat)

Eighth note upbeats on a 4/4 meter:

## 52 | *Applications of Contemporary Harmony I*

Let's take a look at our next melody in F major:

If we analyze the form of this 8-bar melody we can agree that just like on the previous examples, we can divide this into two 4-measure phrases: Phrase A and phrase B.

What we will try to do now is make some of the important melody notes (the ones that are placed on a downbeat and/or the ones that have a longer duration) the seventh degree of a diatonic 7th chord.

On measure 1 we have the melody note E. This note is placed on the downbeat (beat 1) and it has a relatively long duration, so this would be a good opportunity to make that note the 7th of a chord. Then you have to think: Which diatonic chord in F major contains the note E as the 7th degree? The answer will be Fmaj7 (The tonic chord), so we will place that chord on measure 1. So on and so forth. Let's look at a harmonized version of this melody and then I will explain further:

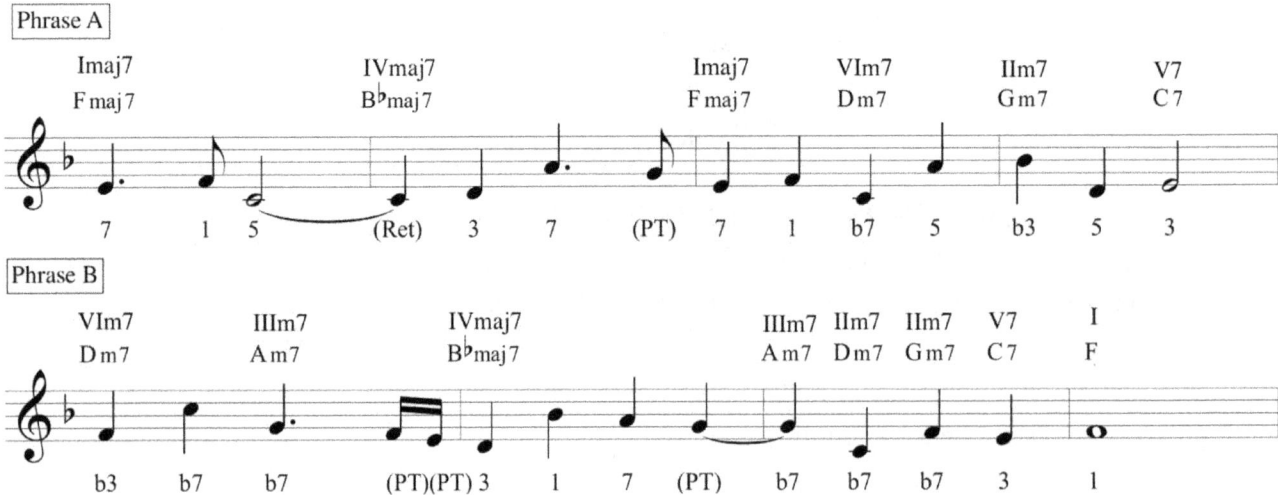

In the following table you can see a measure-by-measure explanation of the note that is becoming the 7th of the chord we harmonized it with.

| Measure # | Chord/s (Harmonization) | Melody Note as 7th degree |
|---|---|---|
| 1 | Fmaj7 | -E (first note of the measure) is the 7th of Fmaj7 |
| 2 | Bbmaj7 | -A (third note of the measure) is the 7th of Bbmaj7 |
| 3 | Fmaj7 - Dm7 | -E (first note of the measure) is the 7th of Fmaj7<br>-C (Third note of the measure) is the 7th of Dm7 |
| 4 | Gm7 - C7 | (NO 7th USED) |
| 5 | Dm7 - Am7 | -C (second note of the measure) is the 7th of Dm7<br>-G (third note of the measure) is the 7th of Am7 |
| 6 | Bbmaj7 | -A (third note of the measure) is the 7th of Bbmaj7 |
| 7 | Am7 - Dm7 - Gm7 - C7 | -G (first note of the measure) is the 7th of Am7<br>-C (second note of the measure) is the 7th of Dm7<br>-F (third note of the measure) is the 7th of Gm7 |
| 8 | F | (NO 7th USED) |

# [3]
# Secondary Dominants

AS STUDIED on chapter 1, the dominant of a major tonality is the 5th degree. In the case of C major, the dominant will be G. If we look at it harmonically, we know that in C major tonality, G7 is the primary dominant of Cmaj7:

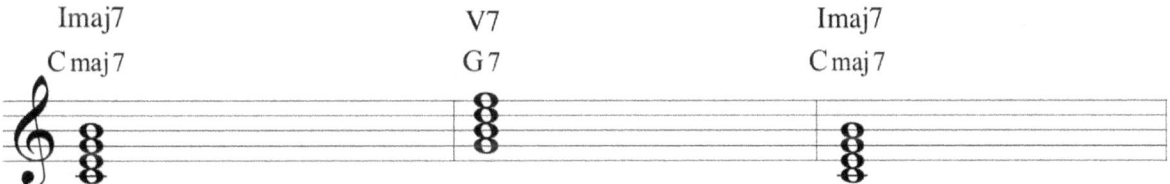

As we've already mentioned on chapter 1, a dominant seventh chord is characterized by the tri-tone interval* (created between the third and the seventh of the chord) in the case of G7, the tri-tone interval happens between the note B (third of the chord) and the note F (seventh of the chord). This is a natural event that happens when you build the diatonic fifth degree chord (Dominant chord) on any given major tonality.

Let's take a look at the intervals created by a dominant seventh chord.

## 56 | Applications of Contemporary Harmony I

This is G7, the primary dominant in the key of C major:

- m3: minor third
- M3: Major third
- +4: Tri-tone (also known as diminished fifth = - 5)

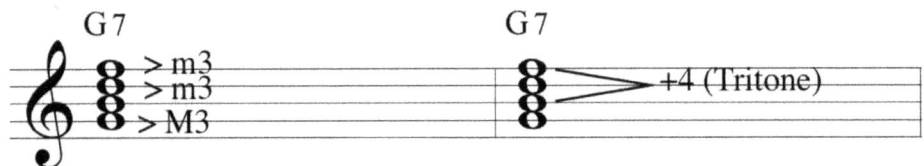

We know that there is only one diatonic dominant seventh chord in a major tonality. When we add the diatonic 7$^{th}$ degree to each of the diatonic triads, this is the 5$^{th}$ or Dominant chord.

> ***Tri-tone Interval:*** *This is an interval of an augmented fourth or a diminished fifth. It's an interval made up by 3 consecutive major seconds (thus, the name triton). It is considered to be a dissonant interval with the need of a resolution.*

A secondary dominant is a chord that will resolve to the other diatonic degrees (just like V7 resolves to I. In C major: G7 resolves to C). This is to say that now we will have a dominant chord (as triad or as seventh) for every diatonic chord on a major tonality.

# Secondary dominant of the second degree (V7/II)

Here are two easy steps to identify and understand secondary dominant on a major tonality:

**Step 1:** Identify the 5$^{th}$ degree of one of the diatonic chords from a major key. For now, we will use C major as an example.

We already know that G7 is the dominant seventh chord of C or Cmaj7, so know let's move to the second degree of C major (IIm7=Dm7). Now we identify the 5$^{th}$ degree of Dm7:

The fifth degree of D is A

**Step 2:** Build up the diatonic chord of the fifth degree:

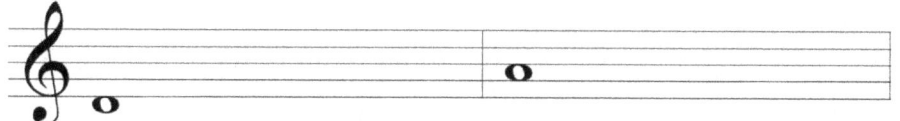

**Step 3:** We identify the note that we have to change in order to convert that Am7 into a dominant seventh chord so that it can resolve to Dm7 (the same way G7 resolves to C or Cmaj7.

We need to take a look at the third and the seventh of the chord. A dominant seventh chord has a major third and a minor seventh (generating a tri-tone between the third and the seventh). Am7 is a minor seventh chord (meaning that the third and the seventh of the chord are minor). We would only need to change the minor third into a major third. The C natural will become a C#, converting the Am7 chord into an A7 chord:

As we can see in the image, the function of the chord has changed completely even though they have the same root (Am7 and A7). This is because while Am7 is purely diatonic to C major, A7 has a non-diatonic alteration (the note C#) making it the dominant seventh chord of the second degree (IIm or IIm7). This is our first secondary dominant in C major and it is called and analyzed as V7/II ("five-seven of two"), which means dominant seventh of the second degree, in this case of C major.

Now we have a chord that can resolve to the second degree by means of the altered third (C# instead of C). It will provide us with a leading tone to D, and the tri-tone resolution (between the C# and G) which will create a need for resolution to Dm:

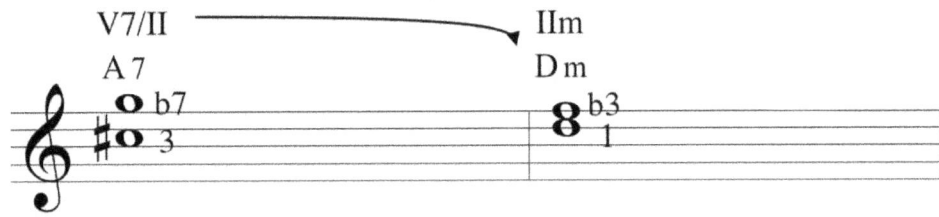

NOTE: Secondary dominants can also appear as triads just like the primary dominant. However, we will continue the examples and exercises using the dominant seventh chords since they appear more often in common practice throughout contemporary music. They both have the same function, the only difference is that the dominant seventh chord will provide a fuller sound while generating the tri-tone between the third and the seventh; which will increase the need for a resolution (the triad does not have this).

In case the A7 resolves to Dm7 rather than Dm (triad), the leading tone C# can actually resolve more efficiently down to the chord tone C natural (7th degree of Dm7). This is because on any seventh chord, the third and the seventh are the most important chord tones since they determine the sound of the chord (we will talk more about this on the "guide tones" section later during this chapter):

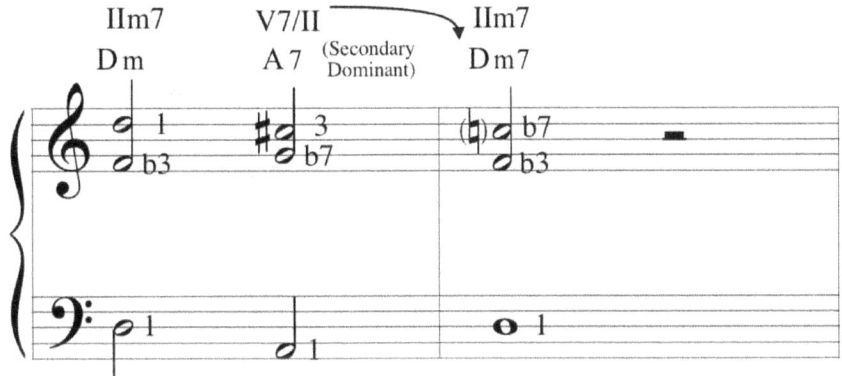

Now let's take a look at a harmonized progression involving the V7/II (A7) in C major.

First, you will see the progression with the diatonic version of the chord (in this case Am7), and then you will see the progression with the secondary dominant:

1)

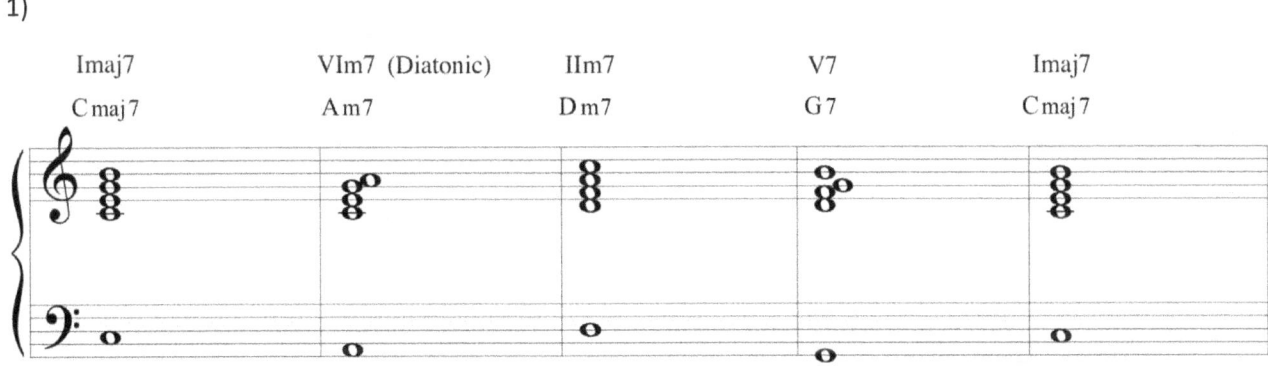

This is a typical diatonic harmonic progression in C major. We start with the primary tonic function chord (Cmaj7) going to a secondary tonic function chord (Am7), then we move to a secondary sub-dominant function chord (Dm7) that goes to the primary dominant seventh chord (G7), and finally resolves to the primary tonic function chord (Cmaj7). We can abbreviate this progression as Imaj7-VIm7-IIm7-V7-Imaj7. This is a very efficient progression since the bass is moving by descending fifths (or ascending fourths) most of the time. Cmaj7 moves a minor third down to Am7; Am7 moves up a fourth to Dm7; Dm7 moves down a fifth to G7; G7 moved up a fourth to Cmaj7.

NOTE: Up a fourth will have the same harmonic result as down a fifth.

E.g.: G7 can move up a fourth to C or down a fifth to C.

Now let's take a look at the same harmonic progression with the V7/II replacing the VIm7:

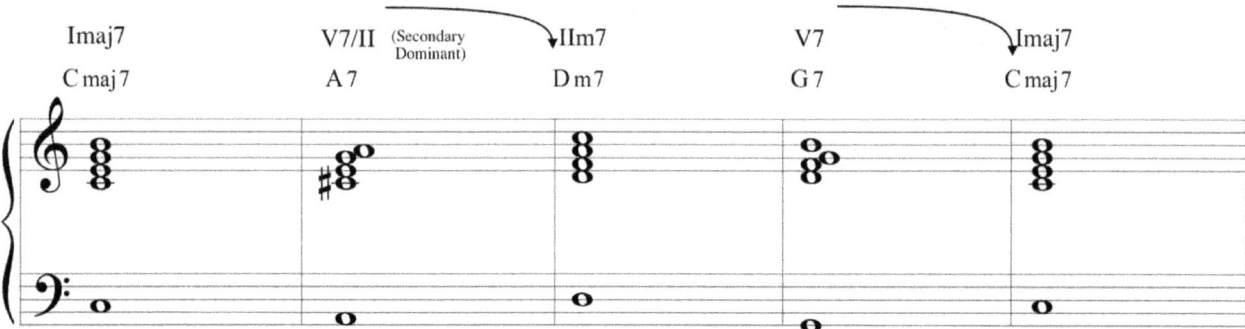

Now you can see how in the second chord, the C has been replaced with a C#, therefore converting the Am7 chord into an A7 chord, which will become the V7 of IIm7. This chord will provide a need for reolution to the Dm chord and will also add an internal chromatic element to the progression. (The chord-tone C moving to C# and resolving to D or to C natural):

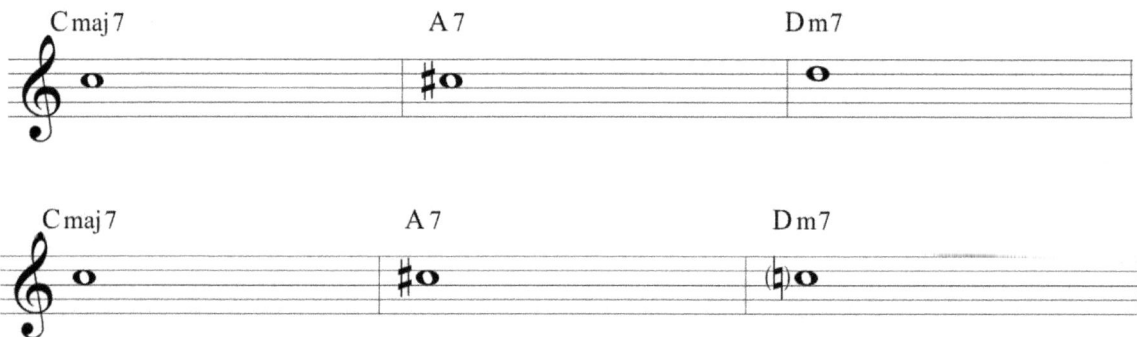

Again, the A7 has a completely different function than the Am7 chord since now it is a secondary dominant.

## Secondary dominant of the third degree (V7/III)

Let's identify the secondary dominant of the third degree in C major using the same three steps as before: 1) identifying the fifth degree of the diatonic chord (in this case Em), 2) building the diatonic chord starting from that fifth degree, 3) identifying the note/s that need to be changed/altered in order to convert that diatonic chord into a secondary dominant chord:

1. Identify the fifth degree of IIIm7 (Em7):

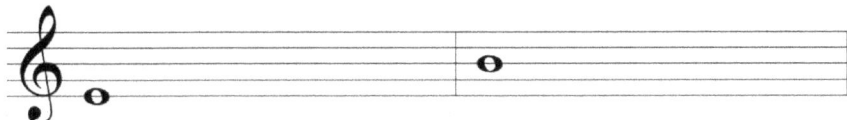

2. Build the corresponding diatonic chord from the fifth degree:

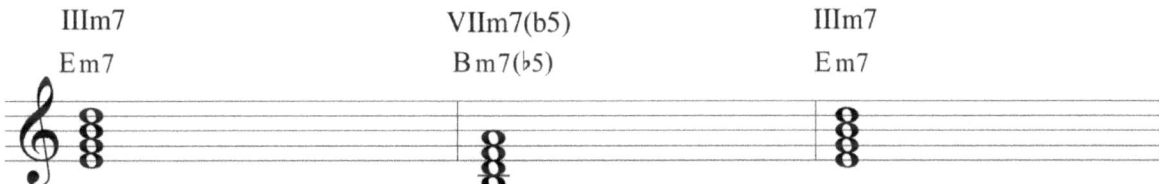

The resulting chord will be a Bm7(b5) which functions as VII7(b5) in C major.

3. What notes do we need to change in order to make Bm7(b5) the dominant chord of Em7?

   In this case we have to change two notes: D to D# and F to F#:

The Bm7(b5) chord changed to a B7 chord which will function as a secondary dominant (V7/III) and will provide a need for resolution to the IIIm chord (Em or Em7).

Let's take a look at a common harmonic progression using the V7/III:

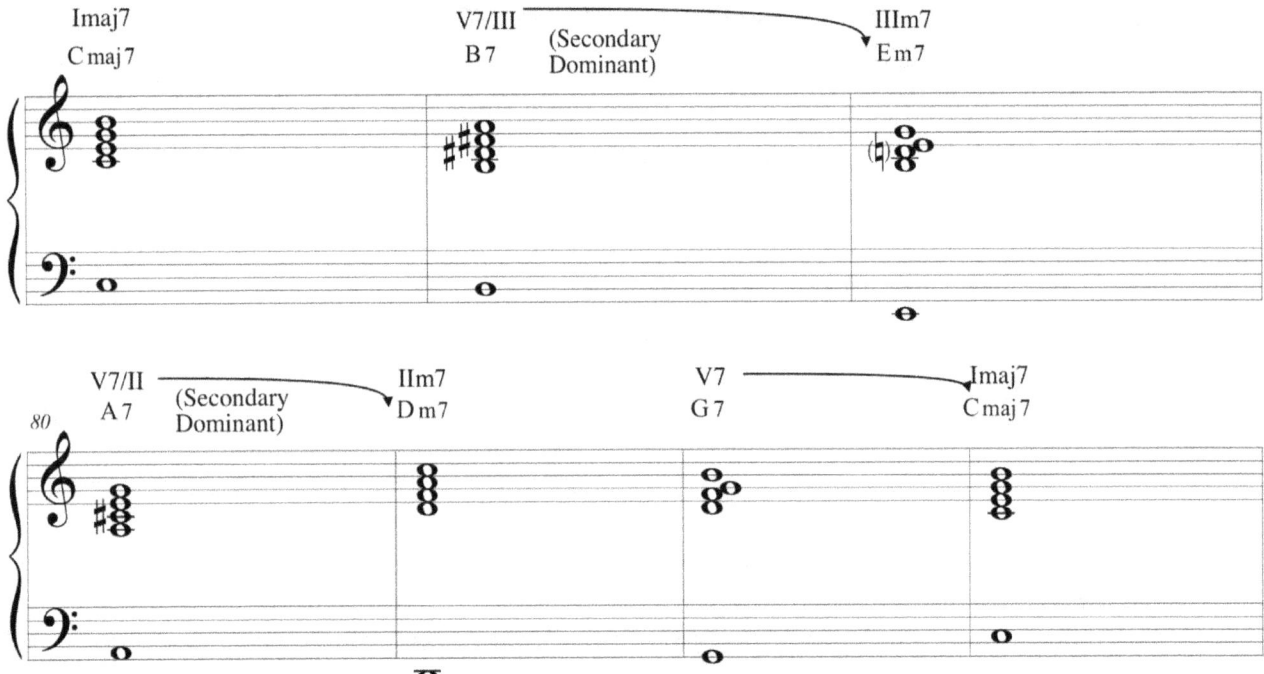

This harmonic progression is moving descending fifths/ascending fourths like the one before. We start with the tonic chord and then move a half step down to the V7/III, which resolves to the IIIm7. This IIIm7 moves up a fourth to the V7/II (A7) and this moves down to the IIm7 (Dm7) which becomes part of a Sub-Dominant to Dominant cadence when followed by the G7; finally resolving to the tonic chord.

# Applications of Contemporary Harmony I | 63

## SECONDARY DOMINANT OF THE FOURTH DEGREE (V7/IV)

The same thing will apply when finding the secondary dominant of the fourth degree. The difference is that now we are resolving to a major chord (Fmaj7=Sub-dominant chord), rather than a minor chord like before.

Let's follow the three steps:

1. Identify the fifth degree of IVmaj7 in C major:

The fifth degree of Fmaj7 will be C.

2. Build the corresponding diatonic chord of that fifth degree:

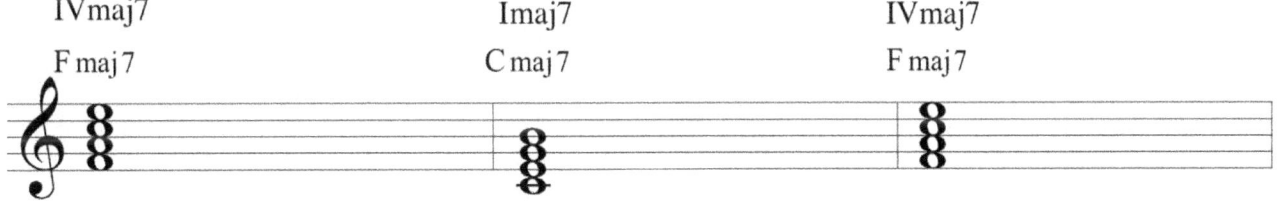

Note that I wrote Cmaj7 down the octave so that it's easier to read.

3. Notes that need to change in order to convert the Cmaj7 into the secondary dominant of Fmaj7:

This time we already have a diatonic major chord (Imaj7), as opposed to the last two secondary dominants which were minor and minor b5 chords before they changed (Am7 changed to A7 and Bm7(b5) changed to B7). Now we have to change the Cmaj7 into a C7. Since we already have a major third in the chord, we will need to change the major seventh degree (B) into a minor seventh (Bb) in order to get a dominant seventh chord (C7):

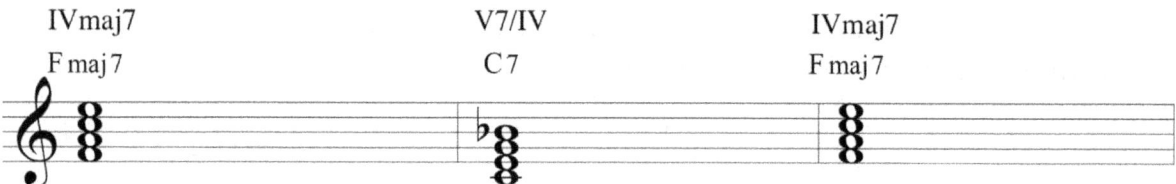

The function of this middle chord has changed completely since now we have the secondary dominant of the fourth degree in C major (F or Fmaj7).

Let's take a look at a short harmonic progression involving the V7/IV:

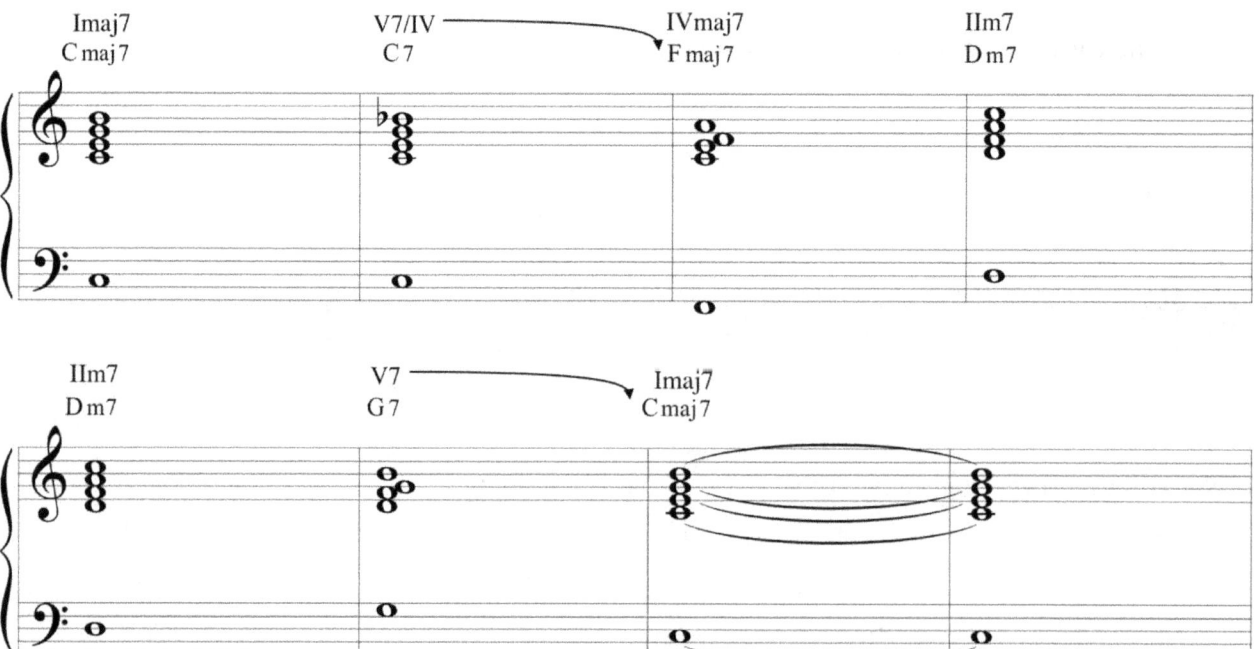

NOTE: the V7/IV has the same root as the tonic of the tonality. In this case C7 (V7/IV) has the same root as Cmaj7 (Imaj7).

## Secondary Dominant of the fifth degree (V7/V)

In this case we will resolve to a major triad (V) or to a dominant chord (V7).

Let's follow the three steps:

1. Identify the 5th degree of V7; In the case of C major, we will find the fifth degree of G7:

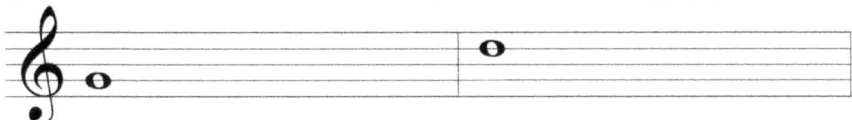

2. Build the corresponding diatonic chord starting from the fifth degree:

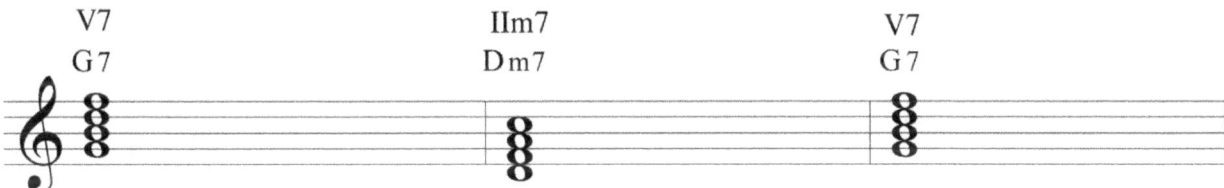

The corresponding diatonic chord is IIm7 (Dm7)

3. Identify the notes that have to change in order to convert this chord into the secondary dominant of V7 (G7):

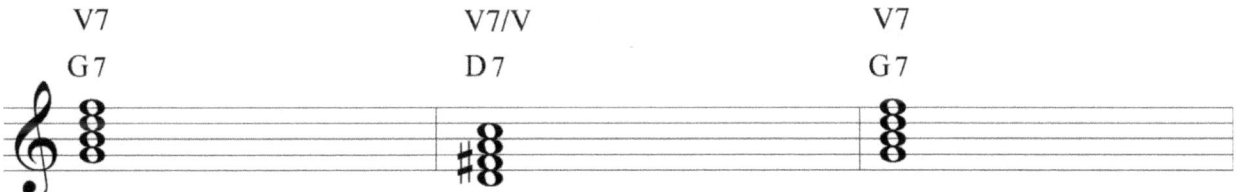

In this case we change the F natural from the Dm7 chord into an F#, generating a D7 chord which will become the secondary dominant of the fifth degree in C major (G7)

Let's look at a harmonic progression involving the V7/V:

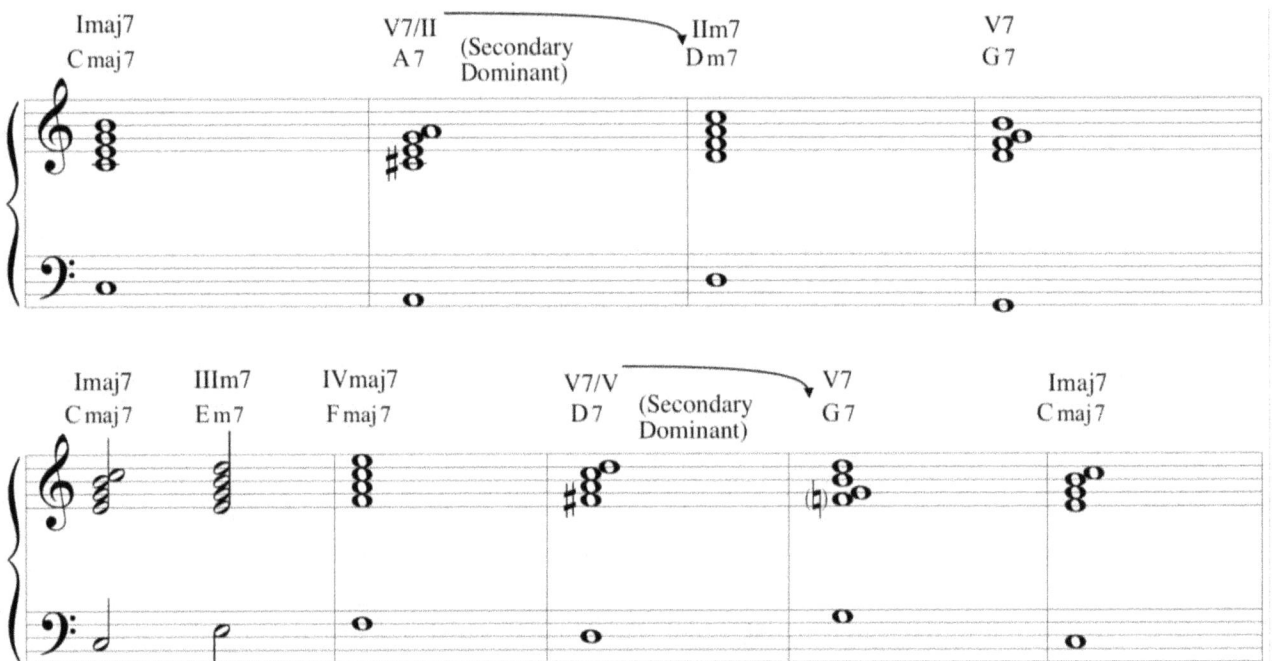

## Secondary dominant of the sixth degree (V7/VI)

This is the secondary dominant that will resolve to the VI degree. In the case of C major it will be the dominant chord that will resolve to an Am or Am7 chord.

Let's follow the three steps:

1. Identify the fifth degree of VIm7 (Am7)

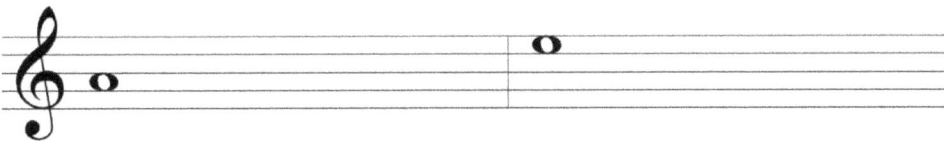

2. Build the corresponding diatonic chord starting from the fifth degree of the VIm7 chord:

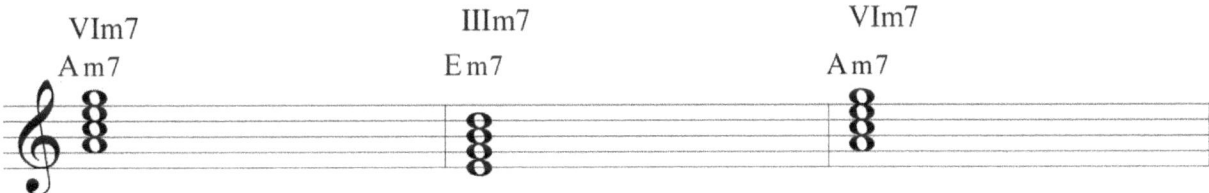

3. Identify the notes that need to be changed in order to convert the Em7 into the secondary dominant of Am7 (VIm7):

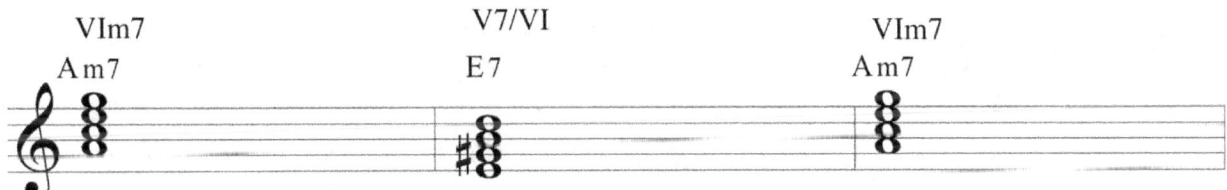

In this case, the note that changes is the G natural (third of Em7) into a G# (third of E7) making the chord the secondary dominant of VIm7.

Let's take a look at a harmonic progression involving the V7/VI in C major:

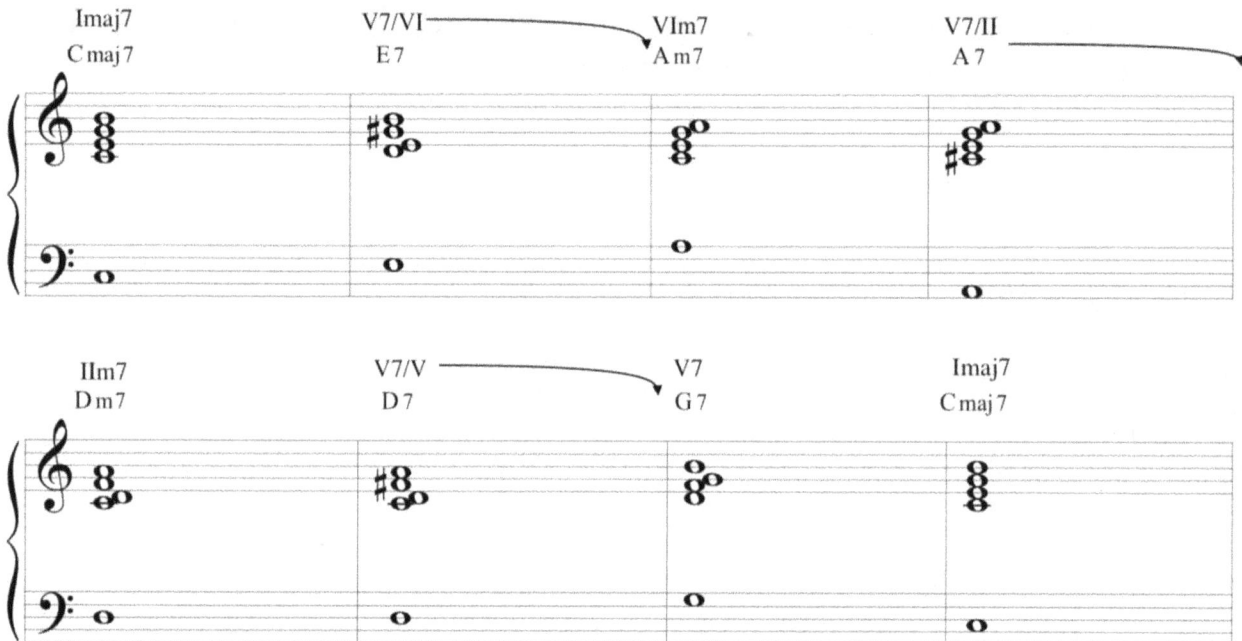

Notice how on every example of a progression involving a secondary dominant there is always a form and a harmonic direction, always starting from the tonic chord so that you can see how these secondary dominants can be presented. This is not done randomly, but in a cohesive way so that it makes sonic sense.

Secondary dominants add a lot of color and expression into diatonic harmony since they generate a heavier sense of resolution to all the diatonic degrees and not just to the tonic degree. Also, the chromatic notes that they provide serve as extremely useful and expressive melodic devices.

Below you can see a table summarizing the secondary dominants on each function in C major:

| Diatonic Chord functions in C major | Diatonic Chords in C Major | Diatonic fifth degree chord | Secondary Dominant of each degree | Function and name of the corresponding dominant chord. | Note that was altered/changed in order to convert the diatonic chord into a dominant chord. |
|---|---|---|---|---|---|
| Imaj7 | Cmaj7 | G7 | G7 (Primary Dominant) | V7 | NO NOTE ALTERED |
| IIm7 | Dm7 | Am7 | A7 | V7/II | C to C# |
| IIIm7 | Em7 | Bm7(b5) | B7 | V7/III | D to D# and F to F# |
| IVmaj7 | Fmaj7 | Cmaj7 | C7 | V7/IV | B to Bb |
| V7 | G7 | Dm7 | D7 | V7/V | F to F# |
| | Am7 | Em7 | E7 | V7/VI | G to G# |

It is very important to understand which note changed on every diatonic chord in order to convert them into secondary dominants because this way you will be able to use those notes as strong melodic devices in your own compositions or arrangements.

As a simple harmonic ear training exercise, try alternating between the diatonic chord and the secondary dominant in order to hear the change of color and function.

This is what you can practice in the piano or guitar (or another harmonic instrument) in order to understand the sonic effect of secondary dominants:

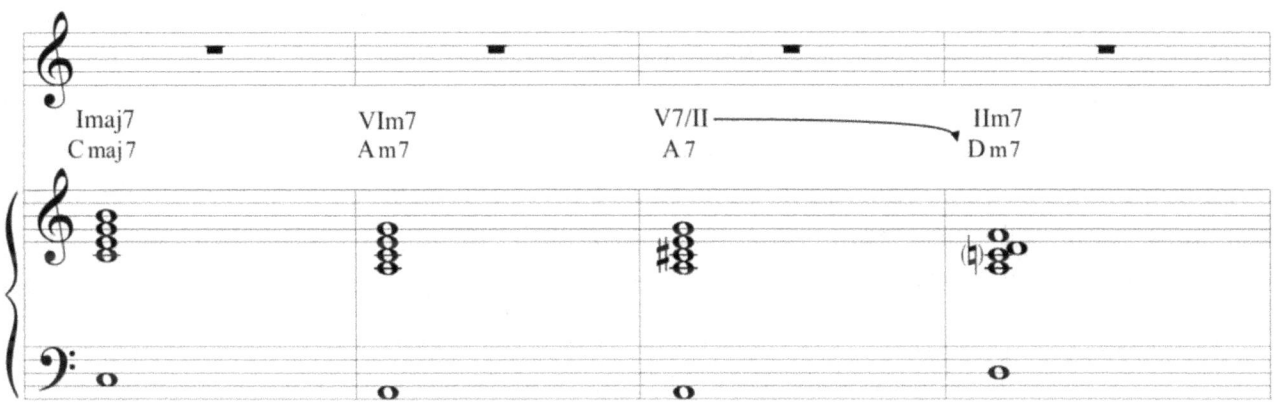

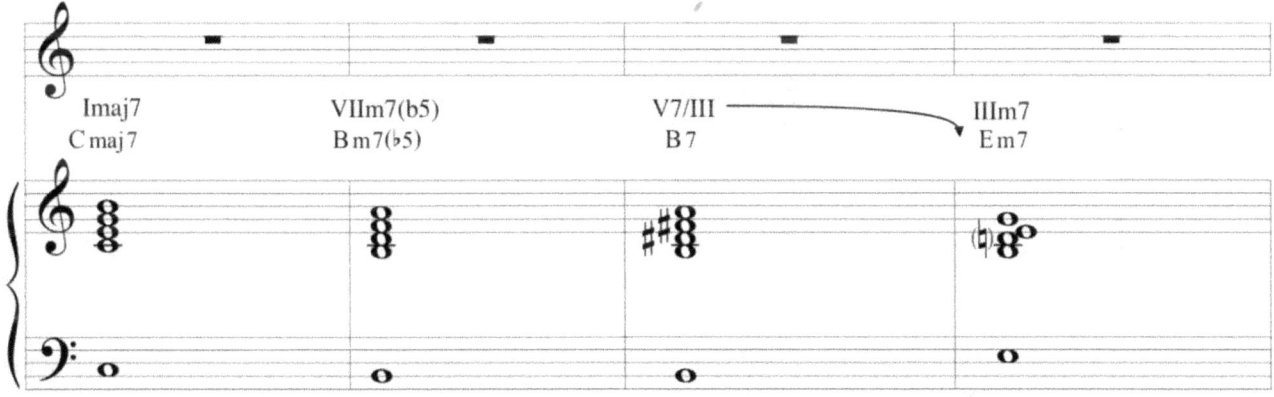

It is always good to start with the tonic chord so that you can hear the functions coming from that chord. You can see in the image that you play the diatonic version of the fifth degree first (Am7 in the first 4 measures and Bm7(b5) in the second 4 measures), and then you change it to a secondary dominant; finally resolving to their respective chords (A7 resolves to Dm7 and B7 resolves to Em7). This way you will be able to hear how the diatonic chord changes its function and color in order to become a secondary dominant. You should do this exercise with all of the secondary dominants and also other chords and functions that we will cover later during this book.

## II-V CADENCES IN SECONDARY DOMINANTS

As we've already studied in chapter 1, a cadence is a musical resolution that provides a sense of conclusion and it can happen melodically, harmonically and rhythmically. All the diatonic cadences that we've studied always resolve to the tonic chord (I) mainly because we only had one dominant chord (V7) in diatonic harmony. However, we now we have five other dominants (V7/II, V7/III, V7/IV, V7/V and V7/VI). Therefore, we can have cadences that will resolve into each one of these diatonic degrees.

In contemporary harmony, especially in Jazz, the most common cadence is the II-V-I cadence which we've already seen in chapter 1. This is a secondary Sub-Dominant (IIm) – Dominant (V) to Tonic cadence. Now, we will evaluate how this cadence can happen on every diatonic degree so that we can have the same cadential sound for each one of them. We've already studied the secondary dominant that will provide the sense of resolution to a diatonic degree; now we will identify the related sub-dominant of each one of them. This basically means that we will have a II-V-I cadence for every degree, but they will not be named with those functions (II-V-I) because they represent another function.

This is a IIm7 – V7 – Imaj7 cadence in C major (Sub-dominant – Dominant to Tonic):

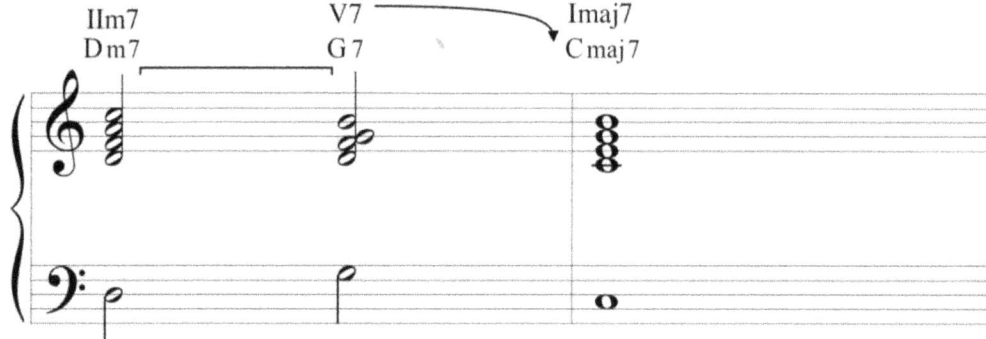

In this image we can see the Dm7 chord being placed in root position moving to the G7 chord with efficient voice leading (maintaining the common notes between the two chords) and finally resolving to the Cmaj7 chord (Imaj7).

NOTE: *The bracket between the Dm7 and the G7 is a symbol that we will use whenever we analyze a II – V cadence in any degree of a tonality.*

Now let's see all the II – V cadences that we can have in C major by resolving to each scale degree with the corresponding secondary dominant (V7/?) and its "related" II (sub-dominant). This means that we will identify the Sub-Dominant – Dominant to Tonic cadence on each degree of the tonality.

# V7/II:

The first thing to do is to identify the fifth degree of the secondary dominant and then build the corresponding minor seventh chord, which in some cases will be diatonic and in others will not.

In the case of the cadence Dm7 – G7 – Cmaj7 (IIm7 – V7 – Imaj7) we know that D is the fifth degree of G and when building the diatonic chord corresponding to the note D in C major, we get a Dm7 chord.

Now let's see how this cadence will look when resolving to the second degree (IIm7) by following these steps:

1. Identify the secondary dominant of the degree: A7 (V7/II)
2. Identify the fifth degree of the secondary dominant: E
3. Build the corresponding diatonic chord starting from the fifth degree of the secondary dominant (E): Em7 (IIIm7) = Diatonic to C major
4. Construct a II – V cadence for the second degree in C major:

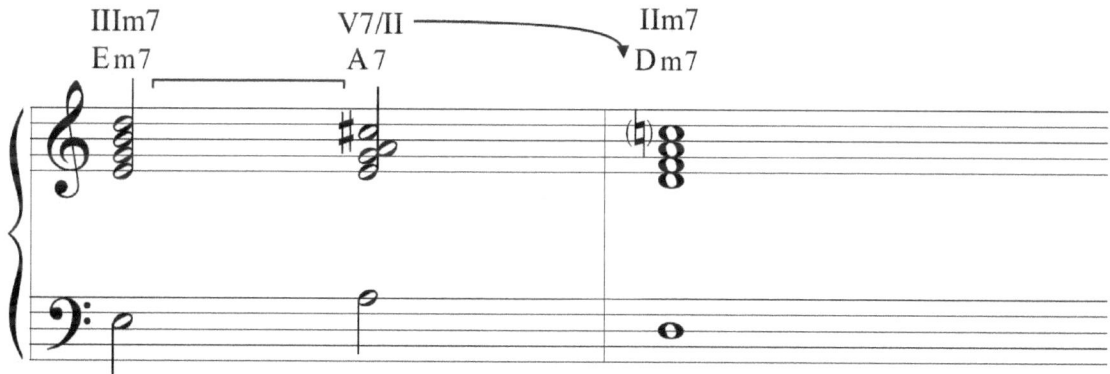

Just like we see in this image, the function of each chord remains the same in relation to C major. However, a cadential sound is being created that will tonify* the Dm7 chord.

Our II – V cadence for Dm in the C major tonality will be IIIm7 – V7/II – IIm7, which is Em7 – A7 – Dm7.

> ***Tonify:*** *To generate a fast sensation of moving to another key by using dominants that will resolve to other chords but the tonic (like secondary dominants).*

## V7/III:

Let's identify our II – V cadence to the third degree in C major:

1. Identify the secondary dominant of the degree: B7 (V7/III)
2. Identify the fifth degree of the secondary dominant: F#
3. Build the corresponding diatonic chord starting from the fifth degree of the secondary dominant (F#): F#m7(b5)

The corresponding "II chord" of Em7 will have a non-diatonic root (F#) since that note is the fifth of B. When this happens, we simply build up a minor chord starting from that note and the result will not be an F#m7 because we would need the note C#, (which is also not diatonic to C major), but it will be F#m7(b5).

NOTE: When resolving to a minor chord by means of a II – V cadence, the "II chord" will usually be a minor seventh – flat five chord ( m7(b5) ) and this will happen as a diatonic result when building up the chord. As a general rule, a II – V cadence that resolves to a major chord will contain a minor seventh chord (m7), and a II – V cadence that resolves to a minor chord will contain a minor seventh – flat five chord.

4. Construct a II – V cadence for the third degree in C major:

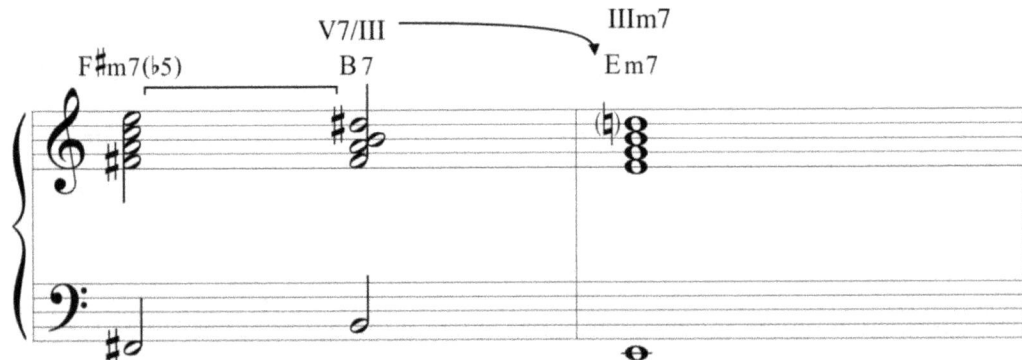

As you can see in the image, the F#m7(b5) chord is not labeled since it doesn't have a diatonic root and hence it is not diatonic to C major. This chord will mostly appear as part of a II – V cadence of IIIm7 (Em7 in C major tonality).

NOTE: F#m7(b5) does have a special function in C major, but it will be discussed in a later topic during this book.

# V7/IV

This II – V cadence will resolve to major (IVmaj7) so it will contain a "m7" chord as the "II chord".

Let's identify the cadence:

1. Identify the secondary dominant of the degree: C7 (V7/IV)
2. Identify the fifth degree of the secondary dominant: G
3. Build the corresponding diatonic chord starting from the fifth degree of the secondary dominant (G): G7

In this case, the corresponding diatonic chord that we build starting from the fifth degree of the secondary dominant of IV will be a dominant chord: G7, so we will have to make a change to the third degree of that chord in order to convert it into a minor seventh chord: Gm7.

4. Construct a II – V cadence for the fourth degree in C major:

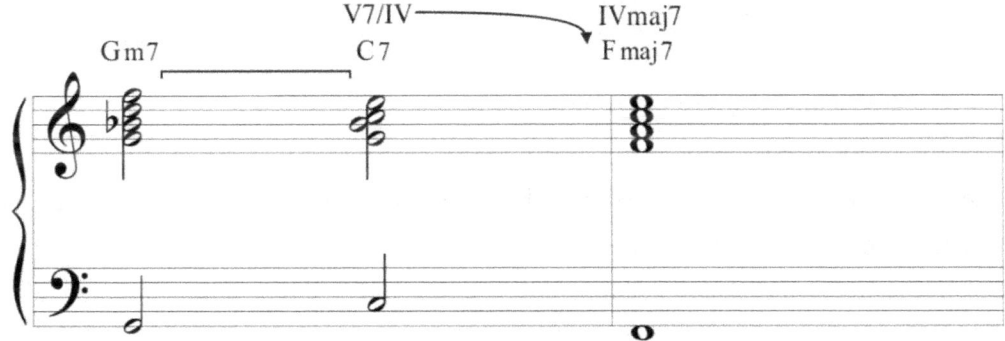

Once again, the "II chord" has not been labeled because even though the root is diatonic to C major, the actual chord isn't since we changed the G7 to a Gm7 in order to create a II – V cadence to the IV chord.

## V7/V

This II – V cadence will resolve to a major triad (V) or to a dominant chord (V7). In both cases the corresponding "II chord" will usually be a minor seventh chord (m7).

Let's identify the cadence:

1. Identify the secondary dominant of the degree: D7 (V7/V)
2. Identify the fifth degree of the secondary dominant: A
3. Build the corresponding diatonic chord starting from the fifth degree of the secondary dominant (A): Am7 (VIm7) = Diatonic to C major
4. Construct a II – V cadence for the fifth degree in C major:

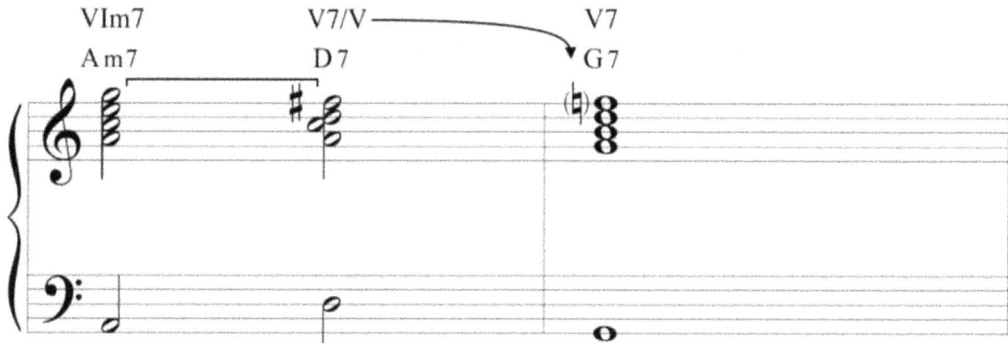

In this case (Just like in the II – V cadence of the second degree) we get a diatonic "II chord" which will be VIm7 (Am7), so it will be analyzed accordingly.

# V7/IV

This II – V cadence will resolve to major (IVmaj7) so it will contain a "m7" chord as the "II chord".

Let's identify the cadence:

1. Identify the secondary dominant of the degree: C7 (V7/IV)
2. Identify the fifth degree of the secondary dominant: G
3. Build the corresponding diatonic chord starting from the fifth degree of the secondary dominant (G): G7

In this case, the corresponding diatonic chord that we build starting from the fifth degree of the secondary dominant of IV will be a dominant chord: G7, so we will have to make a change to the third degree of that chord in order to convert it into a minor seventh chord: Gm7.

4. Construct a II – V cadence for the fourth degree in C major:

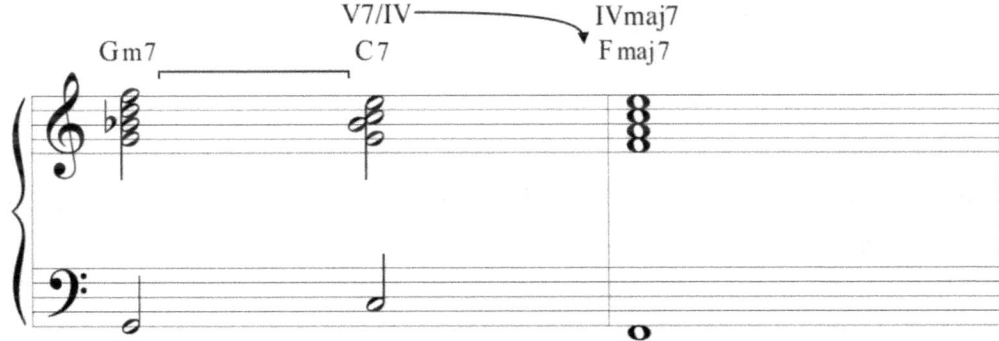

Once again, the "II chord" has not been labeled because even though the root is diatonic to C major, the actual chord isn't since we changed the G7 to a Gm7 in order to create a II – V cadence to the IV chord.

## V7/V

This II – V cadence will resolve to a major triad (V) or to a dominant chord (V7). In both cases the corresponding "II chord" will usually be a minor seventh chord (m7).

Let's identify the cadence:

1. Identify the secondary dominant of the degree: D7 (V7/V)
2. Identify the fifth degree of the secondary dominant: A
3. Build the corresponding diatonic chord starting from the fifth degree of the secondary dominant (A): Am7 (VIm7) = Diatonic to C major
4. Construct a II – V cadence for the fifth degree in C major:

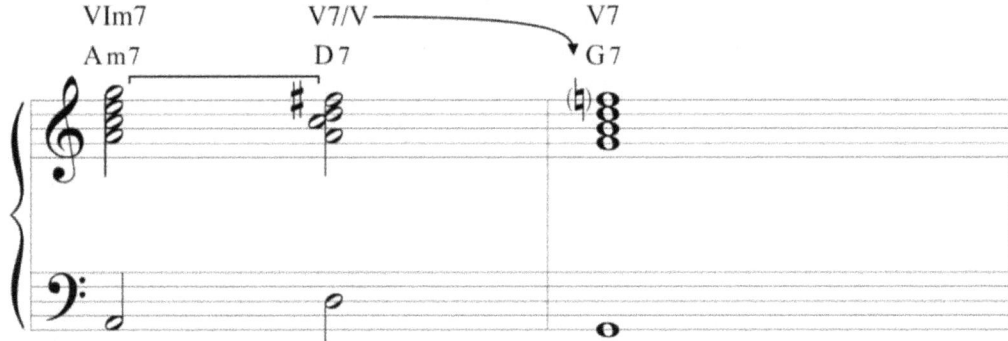

In this case (Just like in the II – V cadence of the second degree) we get a diatonic "II chord" which will be VIm7 (Am7), so it will be analyzed accordingly.

## V7/VI

This II – V cadence will resolve to a minor chord (Am7).

Let's identify the cadence:

1. Identify the secondary dominant of the degree: E7 (V7/VI)
2. Identify the fifth degree of the secondary dominant: B
3. Build the corresponding diatonic chord starting from the fifth degree of the secondary dominant (B): Bm7(b5) (VIIm7(b5)) = Diatonic to C major
4. Construct a II – V cadence for the sixth degree in C major:

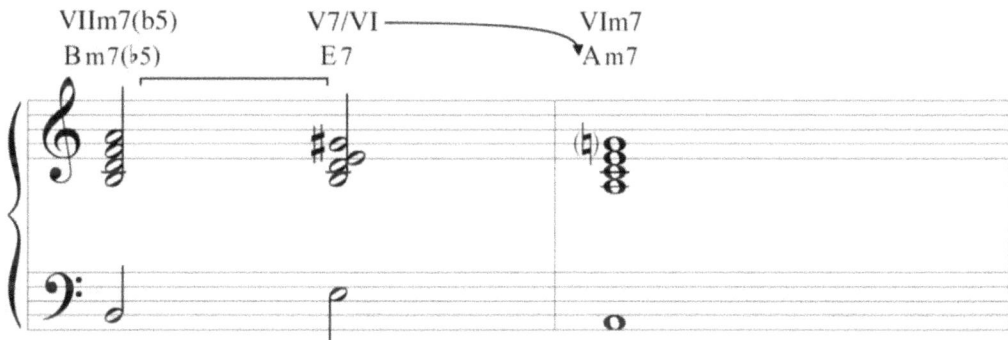

As mentioned before, II – V cadences that resolve to a minor chord will usually contain a minor seventh – flat five chord just like we can see on this image. In this case we get Bm7(b5) as a diatonic result when we build the chord of the fifth degree of the corresponding secondary dominant.

NOTE: The seventh degree of a major tonality does not have a secondary dominant because it is a minor seventh – flat five chord (m7(b5)) and it cannot be tonicized because this can only be done to major and minor chords.

These are all the secondary dominants on a major tonality. Let's take a look at some tables summarizing this topic.

NOTE: you will see three tables of II – V cadences. The first one will contain all the II – V cadences in all the diatonic degrees of C major, the second one will have the same in G major, and the third in F major.

This is something that you must do in every tonality in order to understand the function of the chords visually and most importantly, sonically.

## Table of II-V Cadences in C Major:

| DIATONIC DEGREE | DIATONIC CHORD | SECONDARY DOMINANT | CORRESPONDING "II CHORD" | II – V CADENCES ON EACH DEGREE (FUNCTIONS) | II – V CADENCES ON EACH DEGREE (Chords) |
|---|---|---|---|---|---|
| Imaj7 | Cmaj7 | G7 (Primary Dominant) | Dm7 (Diatonic) | IIm7 – V7 – Imaj7 | Dm7 – G7 – Cmaj7 |
| IIm7 | Dm7 | A7 | Em7 (Diatonic) | IIIm7 – V7/II – IIm7 | Em7 – A7 – Dm7 |
| IIIm7 | Em7 | B7 | F#m7(b5) (Non-Diatonic) | N.F - V7/III – IIIm7 | F#m7(b5) – B7 – Em7 |
| IVmaj7 | Fmaj7 | C7 | Gm7 (Non-Diatonic) | N.F – V7/IV – IVmaj7 | Gm7 – C7 – Fmaj7 |
| V7 | G7 | D7 | Am7 (Diatonic) | VIm7 – V7/V – V7 | Am7 – D7 – G7 |
| VIm7 | Am7 | E7 | Bm7(b5) (Diatonic) | VIIm7(b5) – V7/VI – VIm7 | Bm7(b5) – E7 – Am7 |

## Table of II-V Cadences in G Major:

| DIATONIC DEGREE | DIATONIC CHORD | SECONDARY DOMINANT | CORRESPONDING "II CHORD" | II – V CADENCES ON EACH DEGREE (FUNCTIONS) | II – V CADENCES ON EACH DEGREE (Chords) |
|---|---|---|---|---|---|
| Imaj7 | Gmaj7 | D7 (Primary Dominant) | Am7 (Diatonic) | IIm7 – V7 – Imaj7 | Am7 – D7 – Gmaj7 |
| IIm7 | Am7 | E7 | Bm7 (Diatonic) | IIIm7 – V7/II – IIm7 | Bm7 – E7 – Am7 |
| IIIm7 | Bm7 | F#7 | C#m7(b5) (Non-Diatonic) | N.F - V7/III – IIIm7 | C#m7(b5) – F#7 – Bm7 |
| IVmaj7 | Cmaj7 | G7 | Dm7 (Non-Diatonic) | N.F – V7/IV – IVmaj7 | Dm7 – G7 – Cmaj7 |
| V7 | D7 | A7 | Em7 (Diatonic) | VIm7 – V7/V – V7 | Em7 – A7 – D7 |
| VIm7 | Em7 | B7 | F#m7(b5) (Diatonic) | VIIm7(b5) – V7/VI – VIm7 | F#m7(b5) – B7 – Em7 |

## Table of II-V Cadences in F Major:

| DIATONIC DEGREE | DIATONIC CHORD | SECONDARY DOMINANT | CORRESPONDING "II CHORD" | II – V CADENCES ON EACH DEGREE (FUNCTIONS) | II – V CADENCES ON EACH DEGREE (Chords) |
|---|---|---|---|---|---|
| Imaj7 | Fmaj7 | C7 (Primary Dominant) | Gm7 (Diatonic) | IIm7 – V7 – Imaj7 | Gm7 – C7 – Fmaj7 |
| IIm7 | Gm7 | D7 | Am7 (Diatonic) | IIIm7 – V7/II – IIm7 | Am7 – D7 – Gm7 |
| IIIm7 | Am7 | E7 | Bm7(b5) (Non-Diatonic) | N.F - V7/III – IIIm7 | Bm7(b5) – E7 – Am7 |
| IVmaj7 | Bbmaj7 | F7 | Cm7 (Non-Diatonic) | N.F – V7/IV – IVmaj7 | Cm7 – F7 – Bbmaj7 |
| V7 | C7 | G7 | Dm7 (Diatonic) | VIm7 – V7/V – V7 | Dm7 – G7 – C7 |
| VIm7 | Dm7 | A7 | Em7(b5) (Diatonic) | VIIm7(b5) – V7/VI – VIm7 | Em7(b5) – A7 – Dm7 |

# Applications of Contemporary Harmony I

## APPLICATION

Let's take a look at a couple of short melodies with harmonic progressions that involve secondary dominants and II – V's of Secondary dominants.

For each example, you will see a diatonic version of the harmonic progression first and then you will see how those chords will be replaced with secondary dominants and/or their corresponding II – V cadences.

**Example #1:**

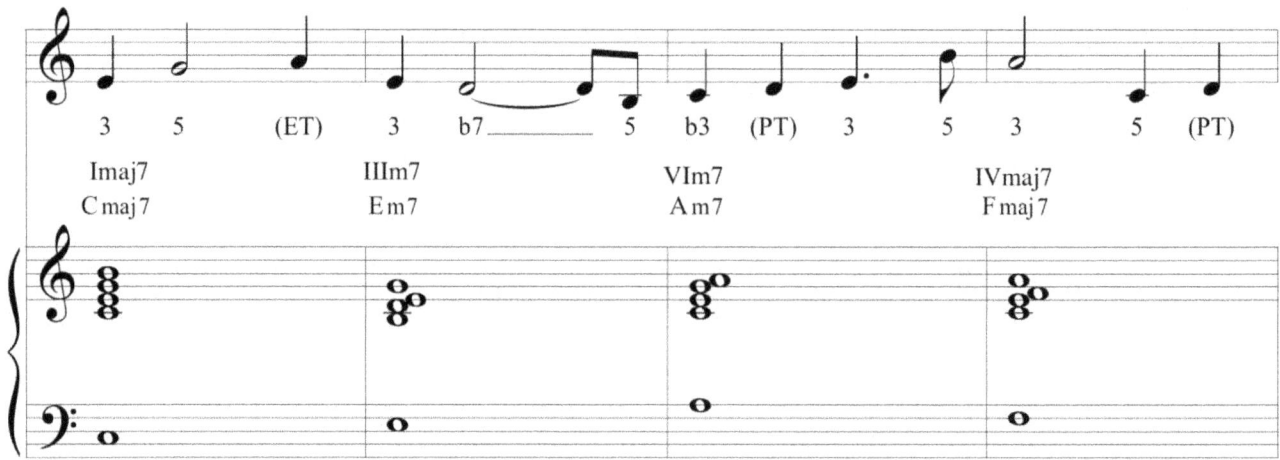

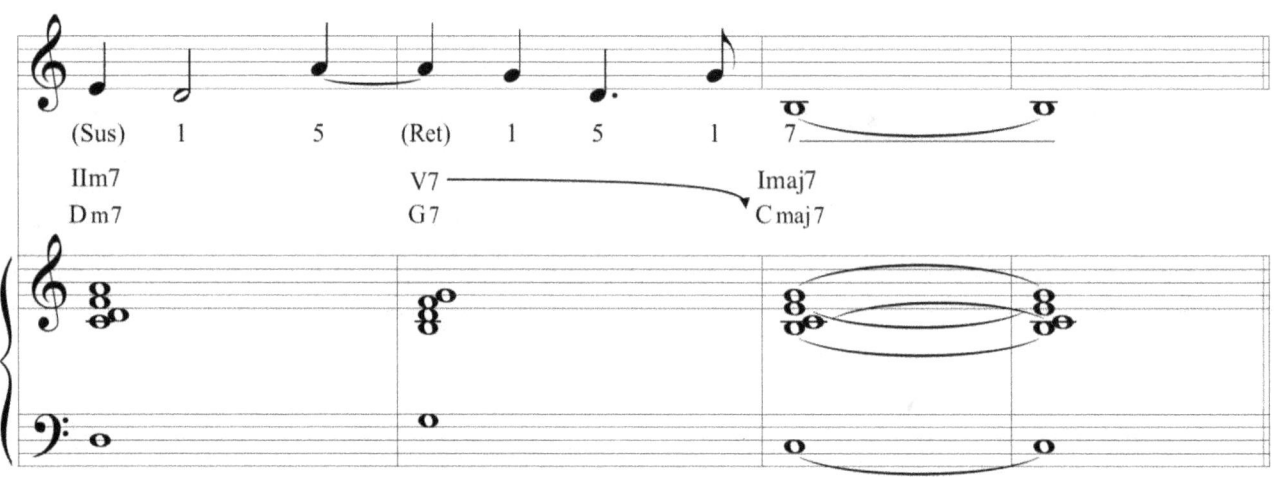

This is a relatively simple diatonic melody with a diatonic harmonic progression in C major. The form of this melody is clearly an 8 measure phrase that could also be divided into two small 4 measure phrases, but it doesn't follow the antecedent-consequent relationship like many of the examples on chapter 1.

Let's do an analysis of the harmonic functions of these 8 measure phrase:

| Chord Symbol | Chord Function (Symbol) | Diatonic Function (Tonic, Sub-dominant or Dominant) |
|---|---|---|
| Cmaj7 | Imaj7 | Primary Tonic |
| Em7 | IIIm7 | Secondary Tonic |
| Am7 | VIm7 | Secondary Tonic |
| Fmaj7 | IVmaj7 | Primary Sub-Dominant |
| Dm7 | IIm7 | Secondary Sub-Dominant |
| G7 | V7 | Primary Dominant |
| Cmaj7 | Imaj7 | Primary Tonic |
| Cmaj7 | Imaj7 | Primary Tonic |

Now let's replace some of the diatonic chords of this progression with secondary dominants in order to create stronger resolutions and provide more movement to the harmonic progression:

## Example # 1.2:

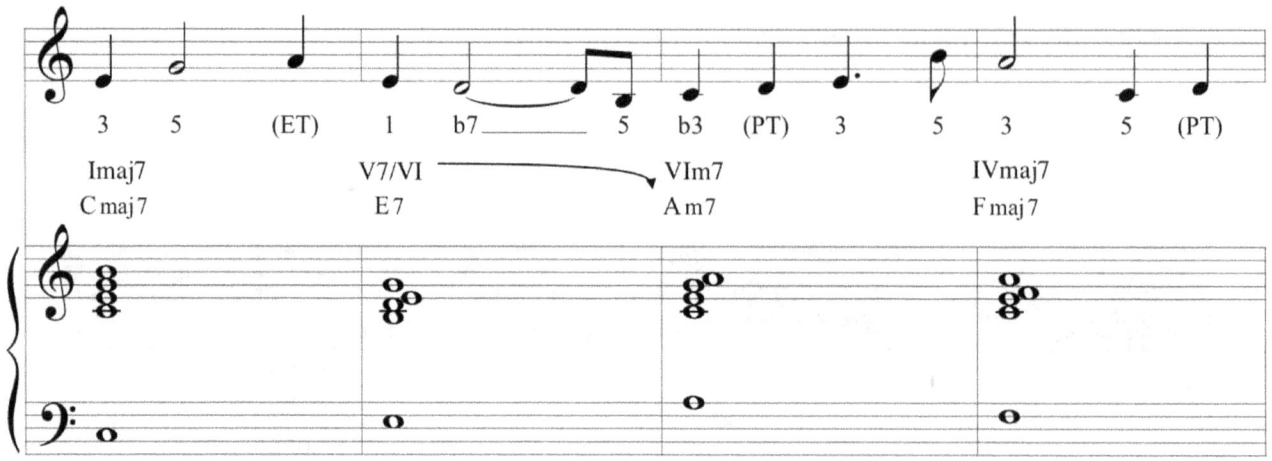

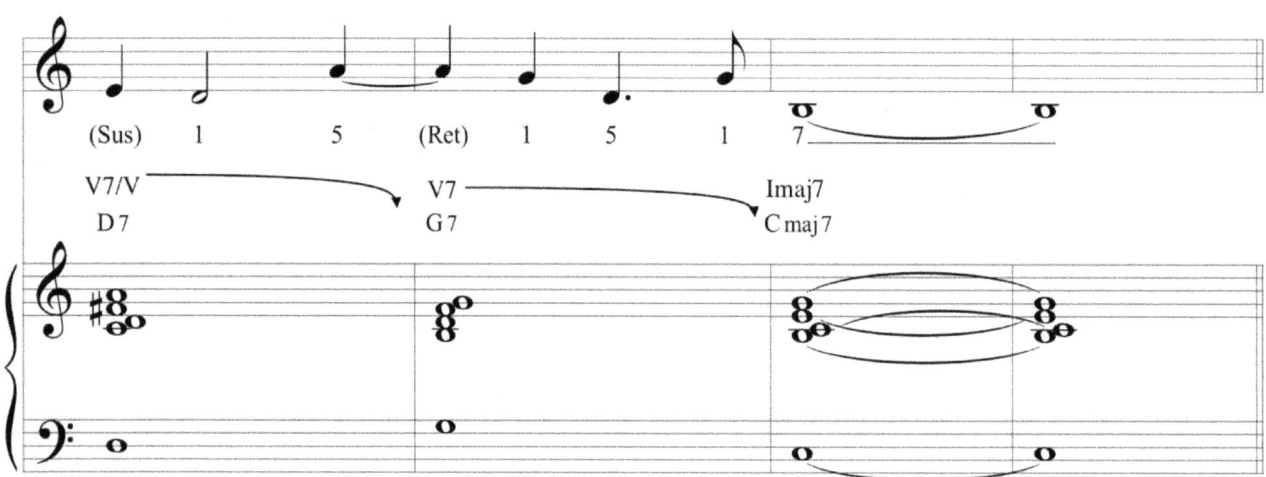

See how the Em7(IIIm7) on measure 2 changed to an E7(V7/VI) and the Dm7(IIm7) on measure 5 changed to a D7(V7/V). This works because the melody notes on both cases also exist in the new chord:

- Measure 2 contains melody notes E, D and B which work both over an Em7 chord and E7 chord since the only note that is different between those two chords is the G#(from E7), instead of the G natural(from Em7). Note that this reharmonization would not work if the melody note on the original 8 measure melody (example 1) would be a G natural because we would have a harmonic "clash" between the notes G and G#.

- Measure 6 contains melody notes E, D and A which work both over a Dm7 chord and D7 chord since the only note that is different between those two chords is the F#(from D7) instead of an F natural(from Dm7). Note that this reharmonization would not work if the melody note from the original 8 measure melody (example 1) would be an F natural because we would have a "clash" between the notes F and F#.

Let's go one step further and add II – V cadences in the same two spots where we switched the diatonic chords for secondary dominants (Note the change of the scale degrees in the melody):

**Example # 1.3**

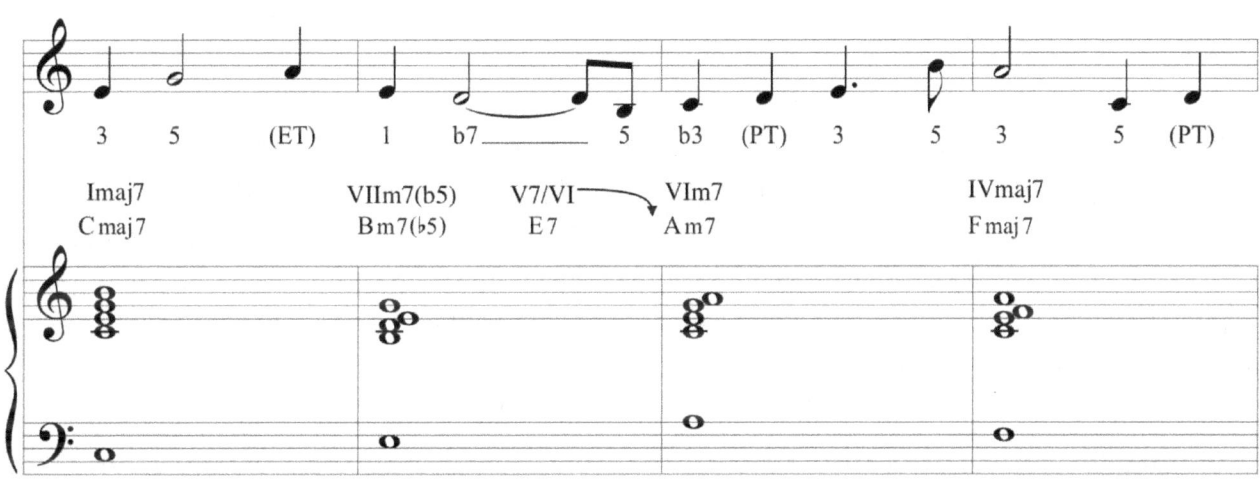

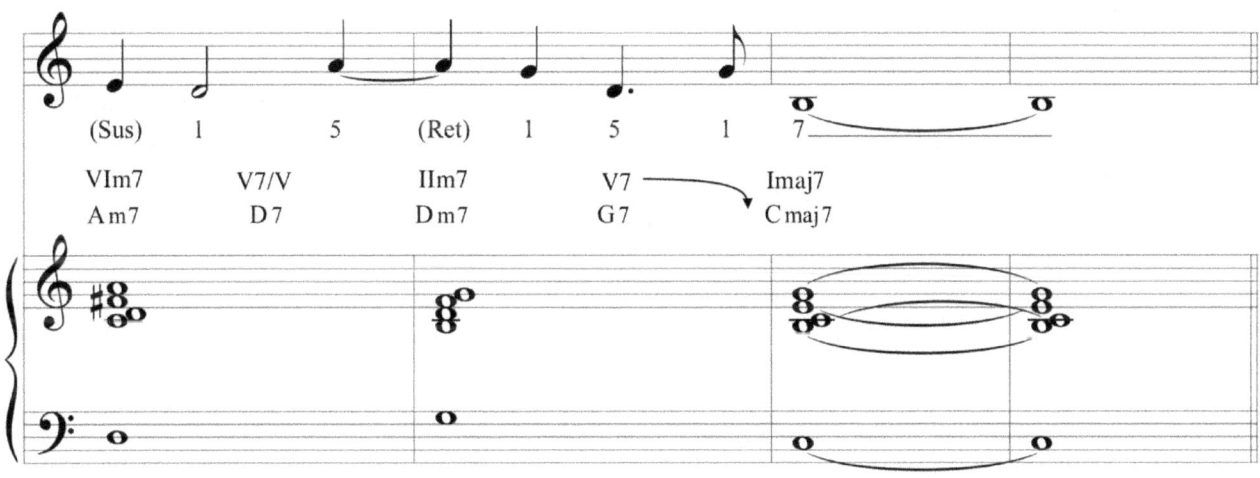

- Measure 2: The Bm7(b5) has been added in the first two beats of the measure in order to create a II – V cadence to the sixth degree of C major(Am7).
  The resulting cadence with their corresponding functions (in relation to C major) will be: VIIm5(b5) – V7/VI – VIm7

- Measure 6: The Am7 has been added in the first two beats of the measure in order to create a II – V cadence to the fifth degree of C major (G7).

In this case, the II – V cadence doesn't go directly to the G7 chord, it goes to a Dm7 chord first and then the G7 chord comes up. As a result, we get two II – V cadences in a row= VIm7 – V7/V and IIm7 – V7 finally resolving to Imaj7. In this case, we say that the IIm7 is an interpolated II, which basically delays the direct resolution of the D7 chord to the G7 chord by being placed in the middle of the two chords.

In example 1.3, you can see how there is still an arrow that goes from the D7 chord all the way to the G7 chord (Skipping the Dm7) which means that the D7 is resolving down a fifth (or up a fourth) to the corresponding diatonic chord eventually. Also, the D7 (V7/V) has a bracket on the functional analysis. This means that the D7 is having a Deceptive resolution which means that a dominant is not resolving directly to where it is expected; it either does it later (like in this case) or it goes somewhere else completely different.

In example 2, you will see a melody that contains some non-diatonic notes (chromatic notes) that will imply specific secondary dominants (E.g.: the note F# in C major will most likely imply a D7 chord). In this case we won't have a version with only diatonic harmony since now it won't be possible due to the chromatic notes in the melody.

This is a 16 measure short song in G major that uses almost all of the secondary dominants. The form on this song is divided into 2 sections (A and B), each one lasting 8 measures (next page):

Page left blank to facilitate chart reading

84 | *Applications of Contemporary Harmony I*

**Example # 2**

# Waiting for Tomorrow

Lorenzo Ferrero

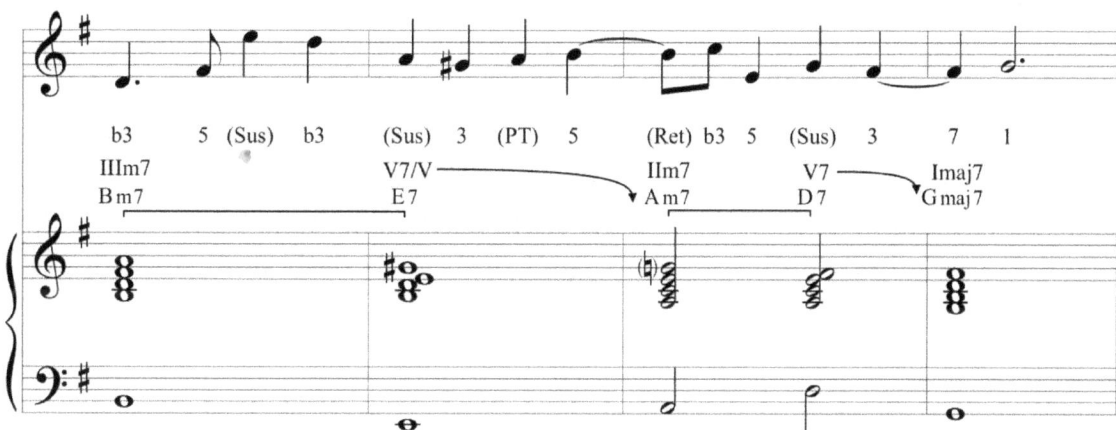

## Guide Tones

*Guide tones* are single lines made out of chord tones that connect a chord progression by the use of efficient voice leading. The most important notes on any given chord are the third and seventh degree because these notes give us the quality of the chord (major 7, minor 7, minor major 7, dominant 7, etc.) The third and seventh are essential when talking about guide tones since they will be based upon them.

Guide tones can be used:

- **To support a melody**: by creating a counterpoint that delineates the harmonic progression.
- **As the core of a melody:** by using the guide tones as a map to direct a melody successfully.
- **As a top note voicing reference**: this is a voicing that is constructed below a specific note provided.

*Guide tones are one of the most basic elements arrangers have at their disposal in order to write powerful lines against a given chord progression.*

The efficient use of guide tones can even make a strange chord progression (made out of functionally unrelated chords) sound good and cohesive.

Let's take a look at the same harmonic progression used in example 2 (Waiting for Tomorrow) against a two-voice guide tone made out only of thirds and sevenths:

Page left blank to facilitate chart reading

# Waiting for Tomorrow

Lorenzo Ferrero

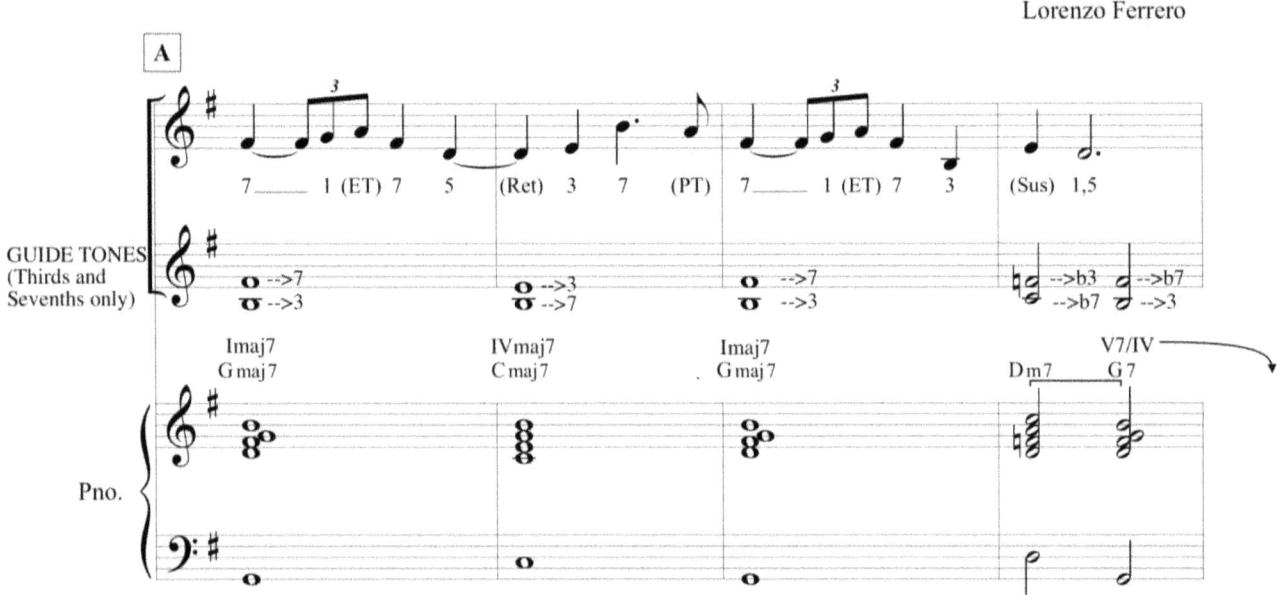
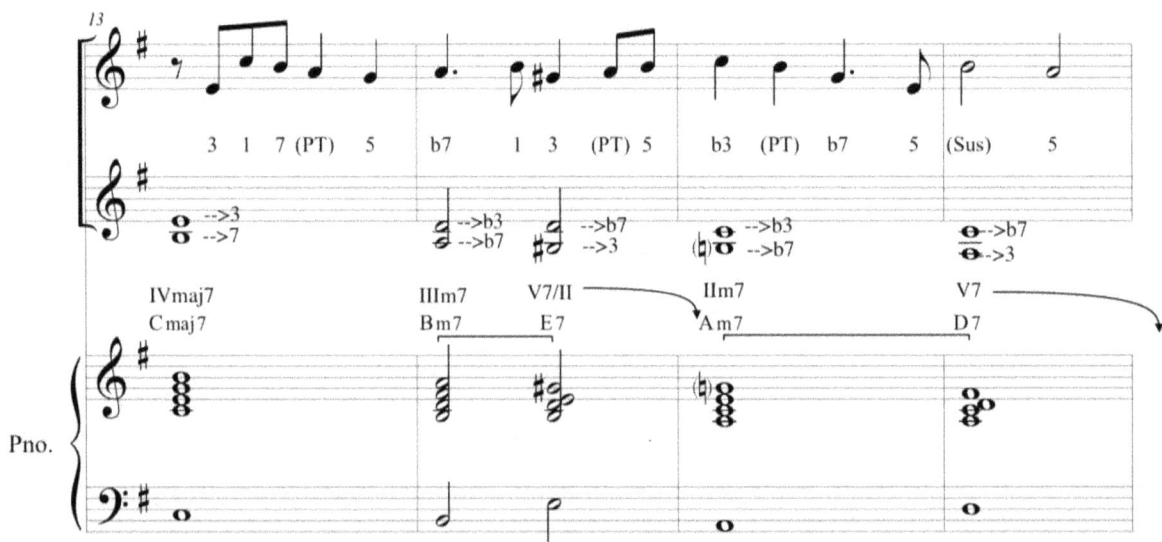

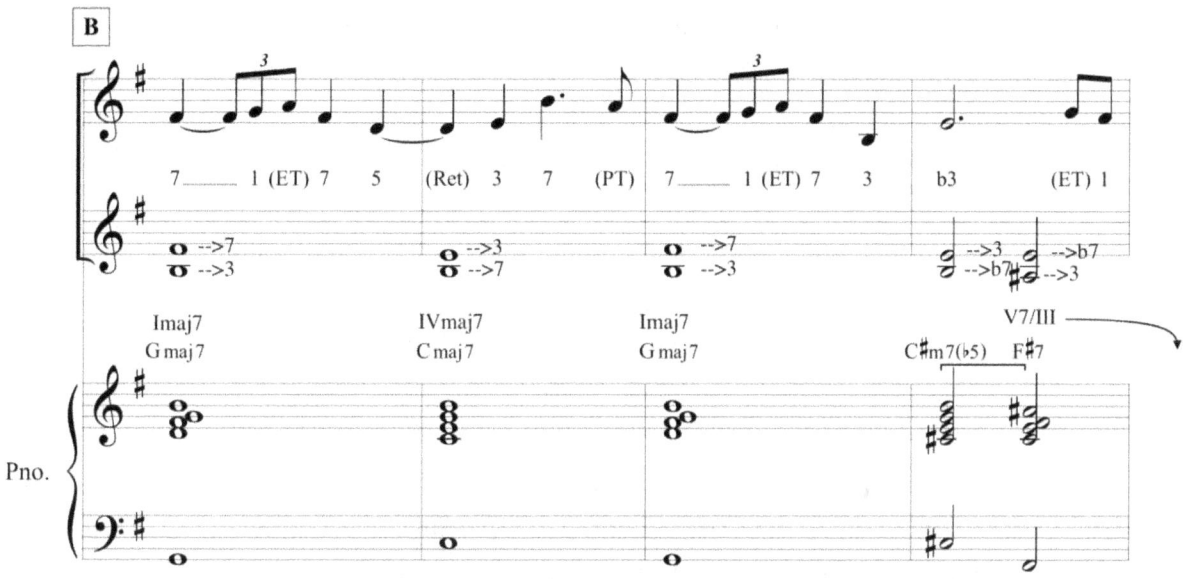

In this example we can see how the guide tones are connecting all the thirds and sevenths of the chords by efficient voice leading. These two notes will provide all the necessary information that we need in order to identify the quality of each chord (major 7, minor 7, dominant, etc.). Notice how in all of the II–V cadences, the third of the "II chord" becomes the seventh of the "V chord" and vice versa; this allows for a very effective voice leading (the least amount of voice movement or none at all)

We will expand the subject of guide tones on *"Applications of Contemporary Harmony II"*.

The following example is a swing tune, which contains some typical Jazz melodic vocabulary. In the example, all of the chords are connected with efficient voice leading, but in some cases I have to re-start the voice leading progression to prevent the voicings from getting *too* low in register (usually an effect of constant voice leading for a long period of time).

The form of the song is AABA, very typical in "Jazz Standards", also very common in pop and many other styles of contemporary music. The AABA form basically consists of two important melodic statements: Section A and section B.

Since section A will repeat three times (with minor adjustments and variations usually at the end of the section to conclude or turn around) it has to contain a strong melody because it will be repeated the most. The B section basically provides something different that will take us away from the melody and harmonic progression of section A; it is very common to modulate in the B section (The subject of modulation will be discussed on a later chapter). This tune will not modulate, it will only contain the topics that we've seen so far.

Page left blank to facilitate chart reading

# Counterclockwise

Lorenzo Ferrero

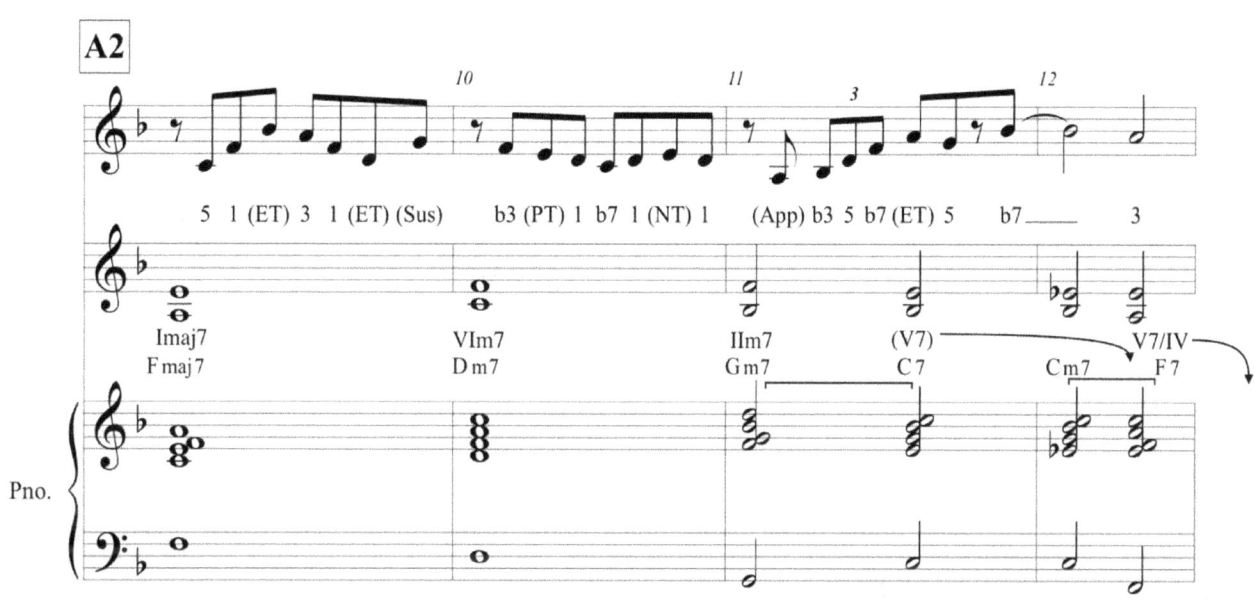

# Applications of Contemporary Harmony I

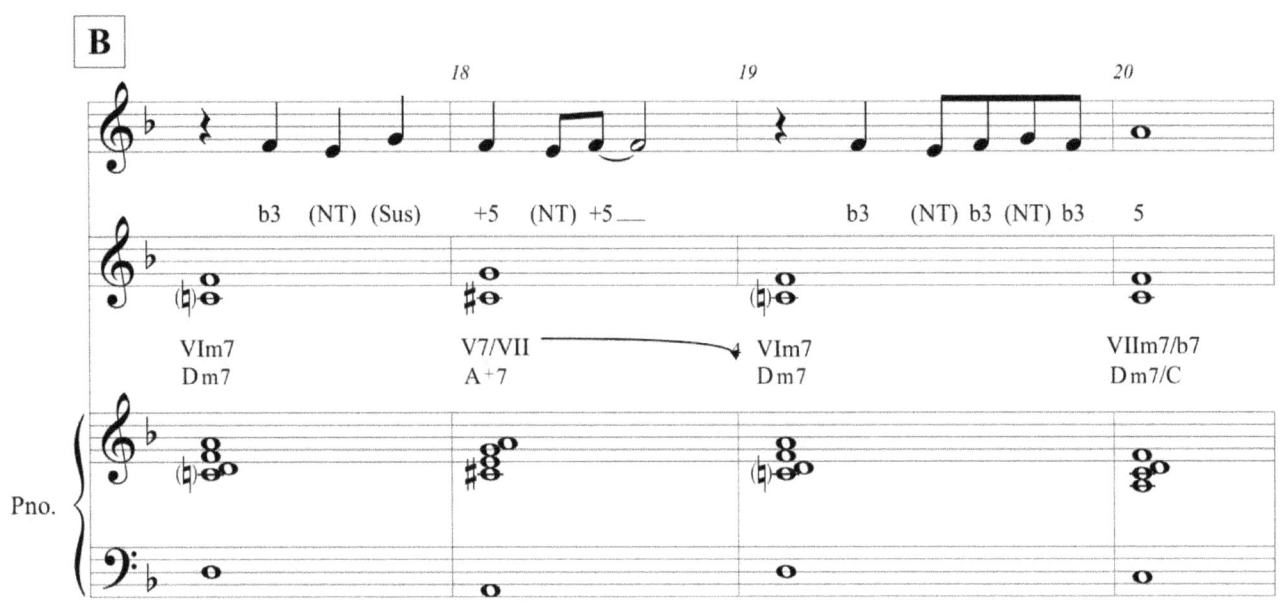

Applications of Contemporary Harmony I | 95

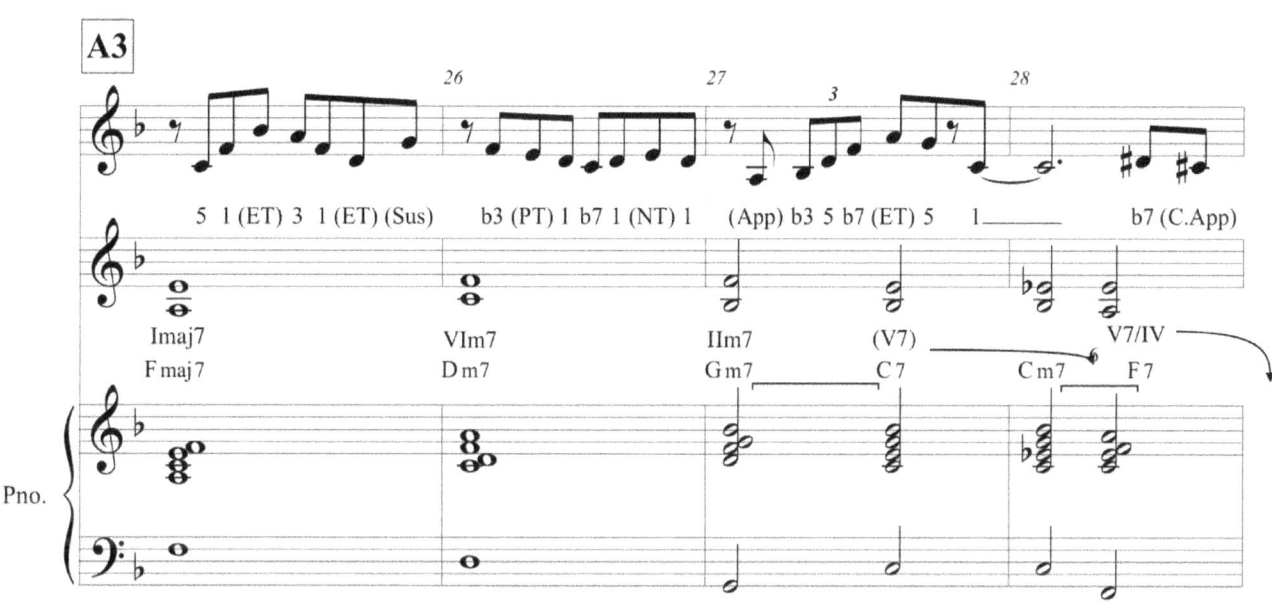

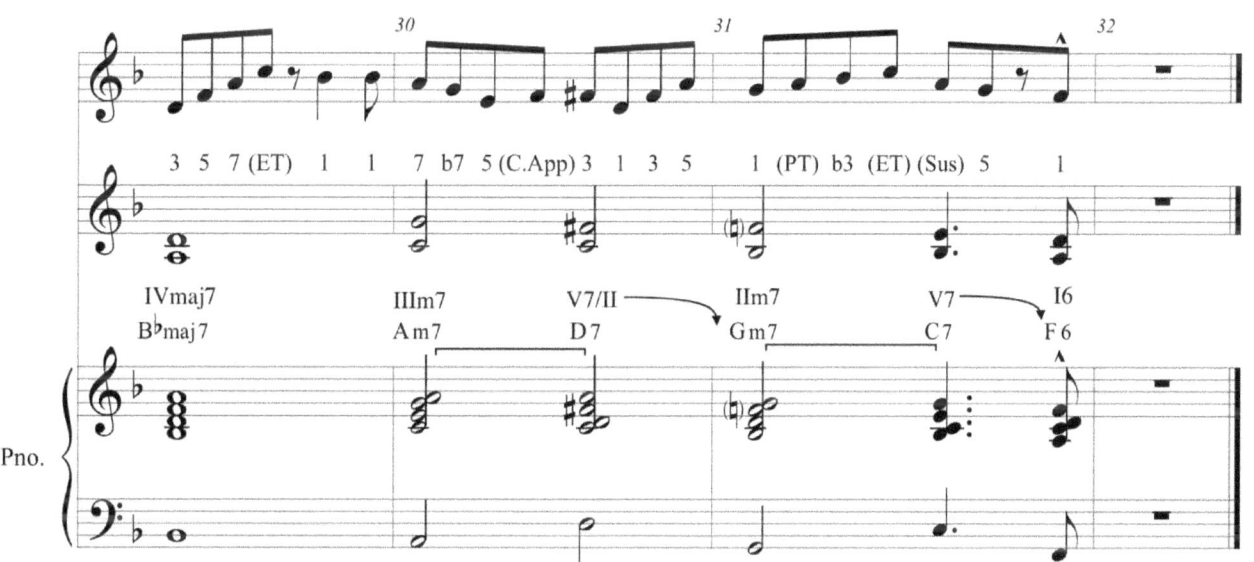

# [4]
# Diatonic Minor Harmony

SO FAR, we have studied all the diatonic functions and secondary dominants in a major tonality. In this chapter we will do the same with the minor tonality.

In chapter 1, there is a brief explanation of the relationship between a major key and its relative minor key, which is that they both share the same key signature, hence containing the same set of notes but with a different functionality.

The relative minor of a major key will be located a minor third below the root (also identified as a major sixth above the root), so in the key of C major, the relative minor will be A minor:

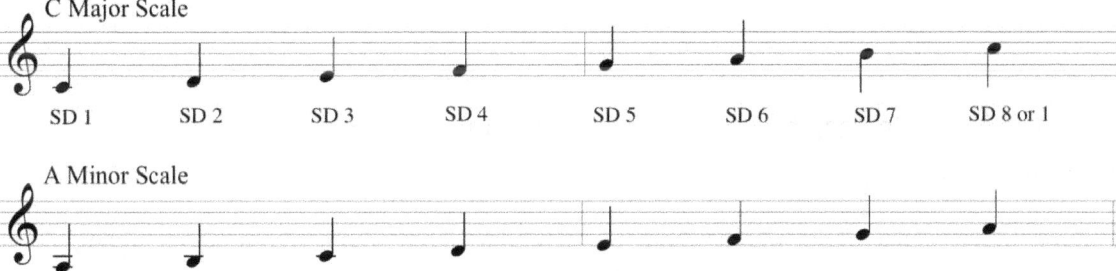

These two keys share the same key signature, they both contain the same notes, but they have different tonics (C is the tonic in C major and A is the tonic in A minor).

There are three types of minor scales: Natural minor, harmonic minor and melodic minor. The minor scale displayed in the previous image is known as a natural minor scale, which has no alterations and has the exact same notes as its relative major tonality.

Minor tonality is much richer than major since we have more diatonic functions, considering that we have three different scales (Natural minor, Harmonic minor and Melodic minor).

## Harmonic Functions in A natural minor:

Let's look and compare the functions of the scale degrees of these two scales (C major and A natural minor):

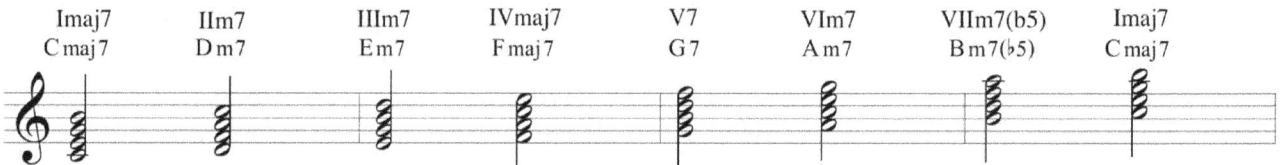

Now let's take a look at the diatonic harmony built on each diatonic degree of A minor:

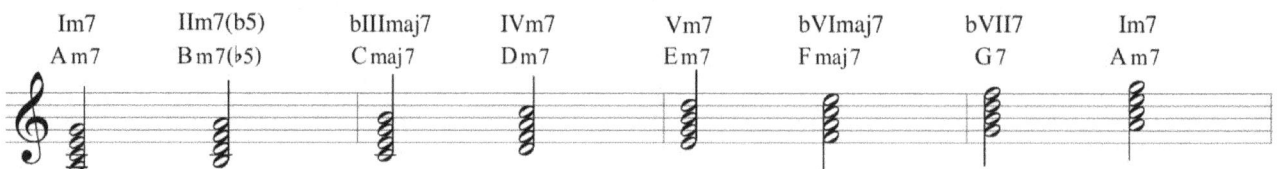

As you can see on this image, the diatonic chords of A minor are the same as on C major, but they have a different function.

*Applications of Contemporary Harmony I* | 99

Just like on a major tonality, we have three main functions in a natural minor scale:

- Tonic minor
- Sub-Dominant minor
- Dominant minor

TONIC MINOR:

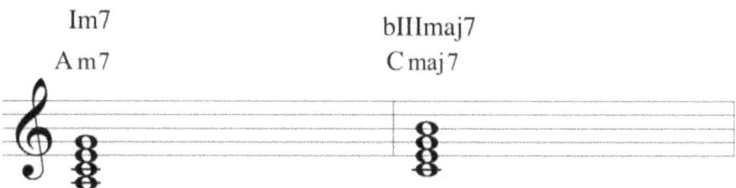

SUB-DOMINANT MINOR:

Observe that the Sub-Dominant minor function has the most amount of chords and that one of them is a dominant seven chord (G7). In A minor (as opposed to C major) the G7 usually resolves up a step to Am7 rather than moving down a fifth to Cmaj7 (this happens in order to avoid tonicizing the Cmaj7 chord since it is not the tonic chord.

DOMINANT MINOR:

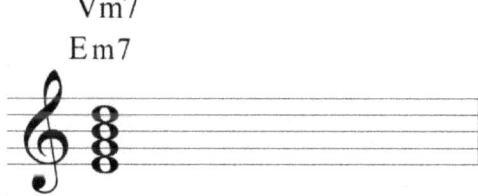

In natural minor, the chord built on the fifth degree is a minor seventh chord (as opposed to the major tonality where we get the dominant seven which resolves to the tonic). In the case of the natural minor scale, the dominant seventh chord belongs to the seventh degree (bVII7), which usually moves up to the tonic chord or moves down a fifth to the bIIImaj7 chord acting as a secondary dominant.

## Harmonic Functions in A Harmonic Minor:

The lack of a V7 chord in the natural minor scale was a big problem because we don't get a dominant chord that will provide a sense of resolution to the Tonic. In other words, we won't get the Leading Tone (the seventh degree of the scale) because in natural minor the seventh degree is flat. In addition, we won't get a tri-tone resolution from an Em7 chord to an Am7; we need an E7 chord. For this reason, the harmonic minor scale was created. This is almost the same scale as the natural minor with one alteration: the seventh degree is raised a minor second above in order to get the leading tone of the scale; in the case of A minor tonality, the G natural is changed to a G#:

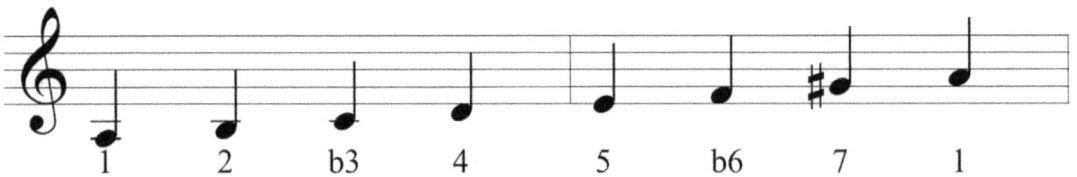

The main reason for changing this note is so that we can have the third of the dominant chord of the tonality= V7 chord (in this case E7) instead of a dominant minor Vm7 (in this case Em7) so that we can get a clear sense of resolution to the tonic and hence getting a sense of tonality. By changing these notes, some of the other diatonic chords will also change their quality.

Let's take a look at the diatonic chords in A harmonic minor:

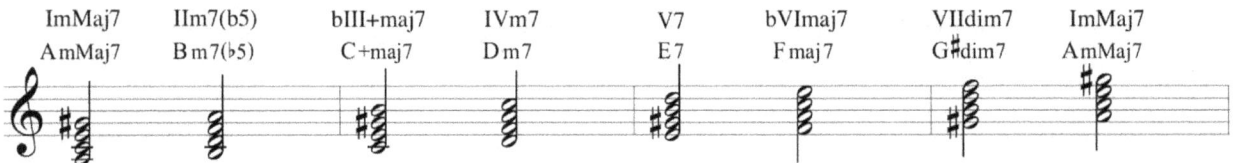

As you can see now we have an AmMaj7 chord instead of an Am7 as our tonic chord. This alteration does not change the function of this chord, it just provides a different version of the same function (in other words, it is still the tonic chord). The bIIImaj7 changed to bIII+maj7 which provides the same function as the previous chord, but with a slight change of color. The Vm7 (Em7) changes to a V7 (E7) which changes the function of the chord completely. First, we had a dominant minor function (which did not provide a need for resolution) and now, we get the dominant seventh of the tonality, which contains a major third and a flat seventh, resulting in a tritone (between the notes G# and D) that will resolve. Finally, the bVII7 (from the natural minor scale) became a VIIdim7.

## Applications of Contemporary Harmony I | 101

### Diatonic functions of A harmonic minor:

**Tonic minor:**

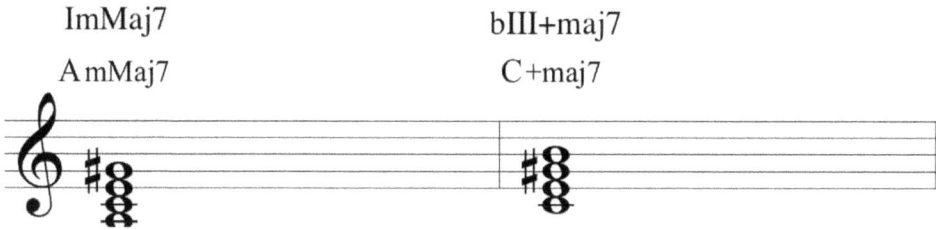

**Sub-Dominant minor:**

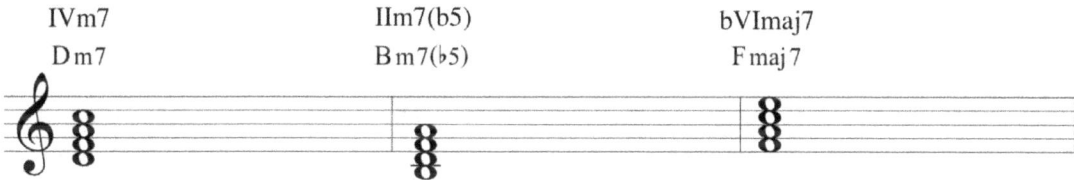

Note that the bVII7 degree does not exist in harmonic minor.

**Dominant Function:**

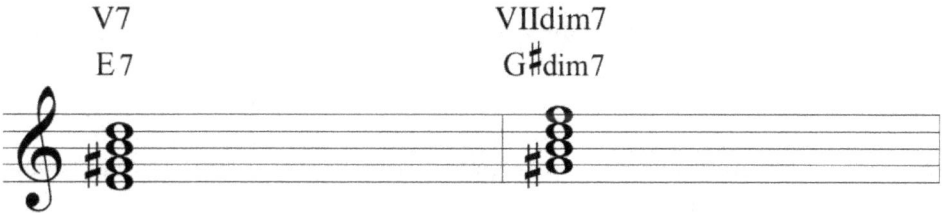

Now we get the dominant 7$^{th}$ of the tonality. (This is a completely different function than dominant minor from the natural minor scale)

## Harmonic Functions in A melodic minor:

This scale is a result of the undesired interval of an augmented second generated between the b6th and the 7th degree of the harmonic minor scale (in the case of A minor, between the notes F natural and G#). I say undesired because in traditional tonal music this was not considered a "western sounding" interval, since it resembled eastern melodic intervals. Even though the harmonic minor scale solved the problem of not having the dominant fifth degree (V7) of the tonality; it was not as efficient melodically because of this particular interval.

The melodic minor scale basically raises the b6 degree (from the natural and harmonic minor) and changes it into a natural 6 (just like in the major scale) eliminating the major second interval from the harmonic minor:

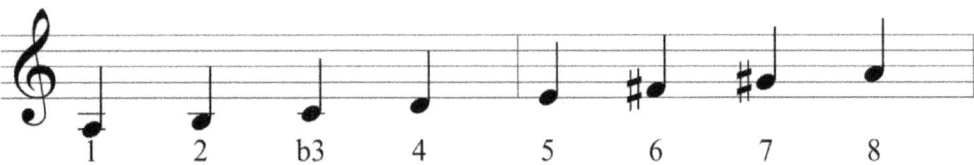

As you can see in this image, the F natural changed to an F# providing a much more melodic tetrachord* than the one from harmonic minor.

> ***Tetrachord**: This is a set of four notes (within the interval of a fourth) used to construct every 7 note scale. It contains a specific combination of major, minor or augmented seconds. The different combinations of notes can give us a major, minor, Phrygian, Lydian, etc. tetrachord. A scale is usually made out of two tetrachords.*

In order to explain the contents of the minor scales, we will need to explain the following tetrachords:

- Major tetrachord: contains two major seconds in a row and one minor second (a major scale is made out of two major tetrachords)

- Minor tetrachord: contains one major second, one minor second and another major second.

- Phrygian tetrachord: contains a minor second, one major second and another major second. (the natural minor scale is made out of a minor tetrachord and a Phrygian tetrachord)

In the case of the melodic minor scale, we can see that it is made out of a minor tetrachord followed by a major tetrachord (note that the second tetrachord of A melodic minor is the same as in A major)

Now, let's take a look to the diatonic harmony of A melodic minor:

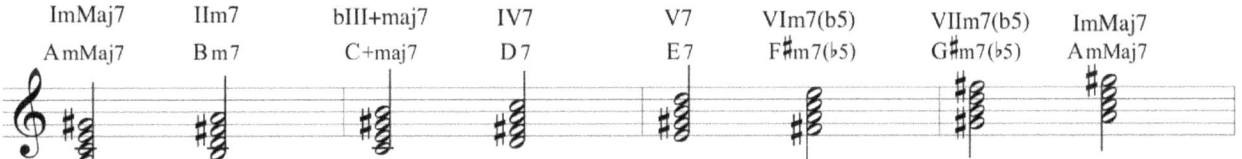

## Diatonic functions of A melodic minor:

### Tonic minor:

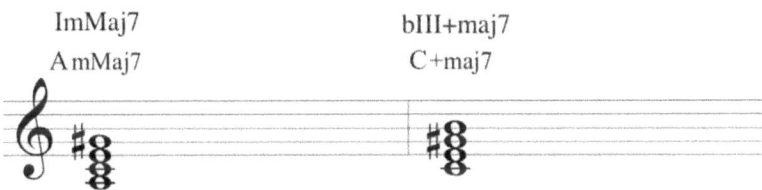

### Sub-Dominant 7th function:

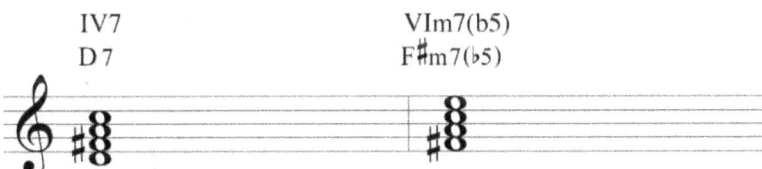

This is very similar to the tonic minor function because the chords in both share most of the notes. The characteristic sound from the Sub-Dominant function is the one given by the natural 6th degree of the melodic minor scale (in the case of A melodic minor the note will be F#). The Sub-Dominant function is usually used right after the tonic minor one, we could say they go hand by hand. This is also a very useful modal interchange device. (This subject that will be discussed in Applications of Contemporary Harmony II).

104 | *Applications of Contemporary Harmony I*

SUB-DOMINANT FUNCTION:

IIm7
B m7

Note that this chord is exactly the same as in A major because of the natural 6th degree.

DOMINANT FUNCTION:

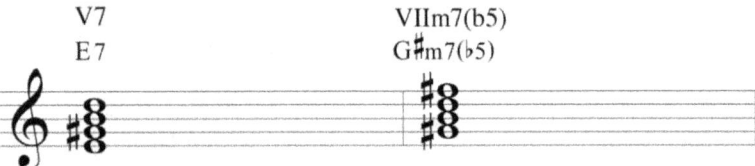

V7                VIIm7(b5)
E7                G#m7(b5)

Note that the G#m7(b5) is exactly the same in A major because of the natural 6th degree.

These are the three minor scales and degrees that should be considered when composing and analyzing a musical piece in minor tonality. As you can see, there are much more diatonic chords in minor (because of the three different scales), than there is in major which gives the minor tonality a richer pallet of diatonic chords to work with.

NOTE: these are two very important musical terms that we will constantly use when talking about minor tonalities:

- **Relative minor key:** It shares the same key signature as its relative major and as a result contains the same diatonic notes but in a different order and therefore different functionality. (The harmonic and melodic minor scales will contain chromatic alterations, which are not part of the key signature)

- **Parallel minor key:** A key that shares the same tonic as its parallel major tonality but not the same key signature; so the parallel minor of C major will be C minor, but C minor is the relative minor of Eb major.

We have used A minor as an example, which is the relative minor tonality of C major. In the following tables, you will see a summary of all the diatonic chords in the three minor scales of this key and then you will see the same thing in C minor, which is the parallel minor of C major and the relative minor of Eb major:

NOTE: In the diatonic function section of the tables you will see the abbreviations (P) which stands for Principal and (S) which stands for Secondary.

A Natural Minor:

| Chord | Functional Representation (Symbol) | Diatonic Function (Tonic minor, Sub-Dominant minor or Dominant minor) |
|---|---|---|
| Am7 | Im7 | Tonic Minor (P) |
| Bm7(b5) | IIm7(b5) | Sub-Dominant minor (S) |
| Cmaj7 | bIIImaj7 | Tonic Minor (S) |
| Dm7 | IVm7 | Sub-Dominant Minor (P) |
| Em7 | Vm7 | Dominant Minor (P) |
| Fmaj7 | bVImaj7 | Sub-Dominant Minor (S) |
| G7 | bVII7 | Sub-Dominant Minor (S) |

A Harmonic Minor:

| Chord | Functional Representation (Symbol) | Diatonic Function (Tonic minor, Sub-Dominant minor or Dominant minor) |
|---|---|---|
| AmMaj7 | ImMaj7 | Tonic Minor (P) |
| Bm7(b5) | IIm7(b5) | Sub-Dominant Minor (S) |
| C+maj7 | bIII+maj7 | Tonic Minor (S) |
| Dm7 | IVm7 | Sub-Dominant Minor (P) |
| E7 | V7 | Dominant (P) |
| Fmaj7 | bVImaj7 | Sub-Dominant Minor (S) |
| G#dim7 | VIIdim7 | Dominant (S) |

Main changes from natural minor to harmonic minor:

There is no dominant minor function on the harmonic minor scale because of the altered seventh degree (in this case G#), which changes the dominant minor function into a dominant function that will resolve to the tonic.

- New Chords: E7 (V7) and G#dim7 (VIIdim7)

NOTE: the AmMaj7 and the C+maj7 are not really considered new chords since their function remains the same.

A MELODIC MINOR:

| Chord | Functional Representation (Symbol) | Diatonic Function (Tonic minor, Sub-Dominant minor or Dominant minor) |
|---|---|---|
| AmMaj7 | ImMaj7 | Tonic Minor (P) |
| Bm7 | IIm7 | Sub-Dominant "major" (S) |
| C+maj7 | bIII+maj7 | Tonic Minor (S) |
| D7 | IV7 | Sub-Dominant Seventh (P) |
| E7 | V7 | Dominant (P) |
| F#m7(b5) | VIm7(b5) | Sub-Dominant Seventh (S) |
| G#m7(b5) | VIIm7(b5) | Dominant (S) |

Main changes from harmonic minor to melodic minor:

We get a sub-dominant seventh function as a result of the natural sixth degree (F#) which will provide new chords: IV7 (D7) and VIm7(b5) ( F#m7(b5) ).

NOTE: There are two chords that are exactly the same as in the parallel major key (A major): Bm7 (IIm7) and G#m7(b5) ( VIIm7(b5) )

Now let's take a look at the diatonic minor harmony in C minor...

# Harmonic Functions in C Natural Minor:

| | Im7 | IIm7(b5) | bIIImaj7 | IVm7 | Vm7 | bVImaj7 | bVII7 | Im7 |
|---|---|---|---|---|---|---|---|---|
| | Cm7 | Dm7(b5) | Ebmaj7 | Fm7 | Gm7 | Abmaj7 | Bb7 | Cm7 |

## C Natural Minor:

| Chord | Functional Representation (Symbol) | Diatonic Function (Tonic minor, Sub-Dominant minor or Dominant minor) |
|---|---|---|
| Cm7 | Im7 | Tonic Minor (P) |
| Dm7(b5) | IIm7(b5) | Sub-Dominant minor (S) |
| Ebmaj7 | bIIImaj7 | Tonic Minor (S) |
| Fm7 | IVm7 | Sub-Dominant Minor (P) |
| Gm7 | Vm7 | Dominant Minor (P) |
| Abmaj7 | bVImaj7 | Sub-Dominant Minor (S) |
| Bb7 | bVII7 | Sub-Dominant Minor (S) |

## Harmonic Functions in C Harmonic Minor:

| ImMaj7 | IIm7(b5) | bIII+maj7 | IVm7 | V7 | bVImaj7 | VIIdim7 | ImMaj7 |
| CmMaj7 | Dm7(b5) | Eb+maj7 | Fm7 | G7 | Abmaj7 | Bdim7 | CmMaj7 |

## C Harmonic Minor:

| Chord | Functional Representation (Symbol) | Diatonic Function (Tonic minor, Sub-Dominant minor or Dominant minor) |
|---|---|---|
| CmMaj7 | ImMaj7 | Tonic Minor (P) |
| Dm7(b5) | IIm7(b5) | Sub-Dominant Minor (S) |
| Eb+maj7 | bIII+maj7 | Tonic Minor (S) |
| Fm7 | IVm7 | Sub-Dominant Minor (P) |
| G7 | V7 | Dominant (P) |
| Abmaj7 | bVImaj7 | Sub-Dominant Minor (S) |
| Bdim7 | VIIdim7 | Dominant (S) |

## Harmonic Functions in C Melodic Minor:

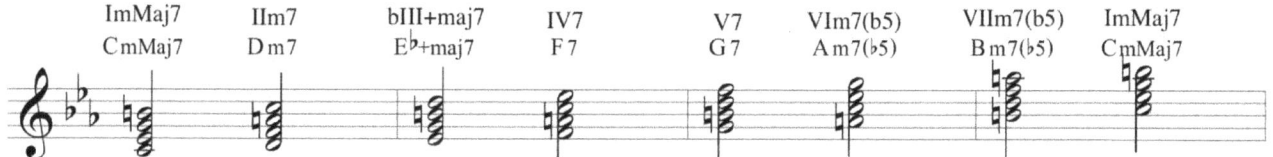

## C Melodic Minor:

| Chord | Functional Representation (Symbol) | Diatonic Function (Tonic minor, Sub-Dominant minor or Dominant minor) |
|---|---|---|
| CmMaj7 | ImMaj7 | Tonic Minor (P) |
| Dm7 | IIm7 | Sub-Dominant "major" (S) |
| Eb+maj7 | bIII+maj7 | Tonic Minor (S) |
| F7 | IV7 | Sub-Dominant Seventh (P) |
| G7 | V7 | Dominant (P) |
| Am7(b5) | VIm7(b5) | Sub-Dominant Seventh (S) |
| Bm7(b5) | VIIm7(b5) | Dominant (S) |

## Secondary Dominants and II-V cadences in minor tonality:

Secondary dominants in a minor tonality are built the same way as in a major tonality.

First we identify the fifth degree of every diatonic degree in the minor scale and then we change (if needed) the third or seventh of the chord in order to make it a dominant seventh.

Let's identify the secondary dominants of all the diatonic degrees of C minor (natural, harmonic and melodic) by using the same three steps as we used on chapter 3:

1. Identify the fifth degree of the diatonic degree
2. Build the corresponding diatonic chord of that fifth degree
3. Identify the note(s) that have to change in order to convert that chord into a dominant seventh.

After that we will identify the corresponding "II chord" of each of the secondary dominants in order to create a II-V cadence for each degree of a minor key.

[Here is a small review of chapter 3: Remember that the "II chord" of a II-V cadence is a chord built from the fifth degree of the corresponding secondary dominant (or the second degree of the corresponding resolution):

In C major, the secondary dominant of Dm7 (IIm7) is A7 (V7/II). To identify the "II chord" in order to create a II-V progression that resolves to Dm7 we simply identify the fifth degree of A7, which will be the note E, or we can also get the same result by looking at it as the second degree of Dm7; both will give you the same result. After that, we build the corresponding minor chord and verify if it's diatonic or not. Since we are in C major, we can keep the Em7 chord as the "II chord" of Dm7 and its corresponding analysis will be IIIm7.

As a general use in contemporary music, the II-V cadences that resolve to a major chord contain a minor seventh (m7) "II chord" and the ones that resolve to a minor chord will contain a minor seventh flat five (m7(b5)) "II chord". This will mostly be a diatonic result with some exceptions (like in the previous example, we get an Em7 instead of an Em7(b5) as the "II chord" of Dm7 in the key of C major because Em7 is diatonic to that key and Em7(b5) is not. In Applications of Contemporary Harmony II we will discuss this topic further and we will see all the possibilities and combinations of II-V cadences.]

In a minor tonality, we get the dominant seventh chord from the harmonic or melodic minor scales since the diatonic chord of the fifth degree in the natural minor scale is a dominant minor chord that will not provide any resolution to the Tonic.

So, if we are in C minor, the dominant seventh chord will be G7, which comes from C harmonic/melodic minor:

Corresponding II-V cadence:

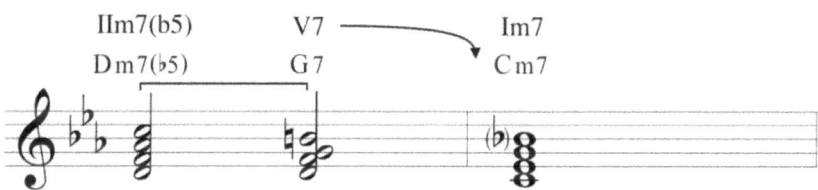

## SECONDARY DOMINANT OF THE SECOND DEGREE (V7/II):

As we've already seen before, there are two different chords for the second degree on a minor scale. The first one is a IIm7(b5) which comes from the natural and harmonic minor scale, and the second one is a IIm7 (the same as in the parallel major tonality) which comes from the melodic minor scale. The corresponding secondary dominant will be A7:

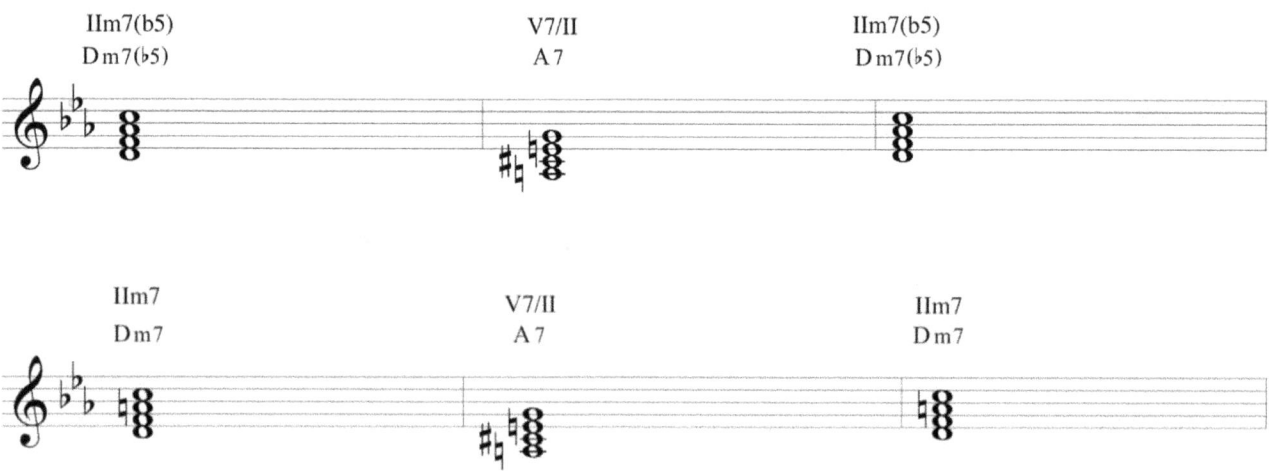

Corresponding II-V cadence:

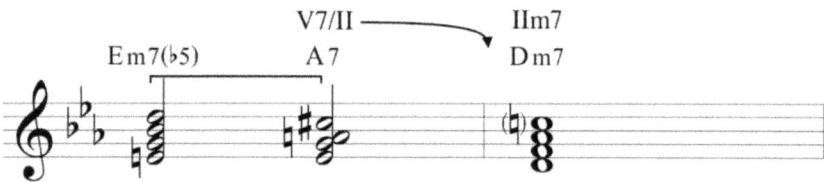

Notice that the Em7(b5) doesn't have any analysis because it is not diatonic to any of the three C minor scales. It only serves as part of this II-V cadence being the second degree of Dm7 (also fifth degree of A7).

## Secondary Dominant of the Flat Three Degree (V7/bIII or bVII7):

The bIIImaj7 degree corresponds to the relative major tonality, which contains the same key signature as its relative minor. In this case, the corresponding secondary dominant will be a diatonic chord: The bVII7, which will act as a five seven of flat three (V7/bIII) but since the chord is diatonic to C minor (coming from C natural minor) the analysis will stay as bVII7.

This is also a V-I cadence in Eb major, which is the relative major tonality.

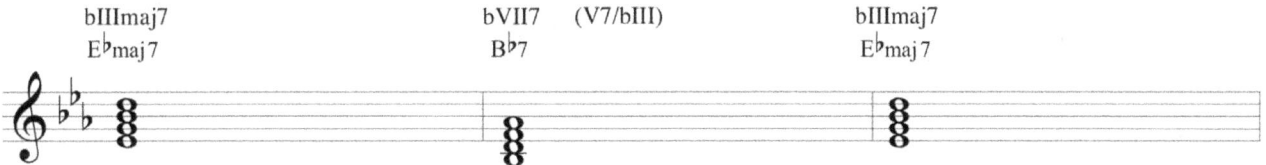

Corresponding II-V cadence:

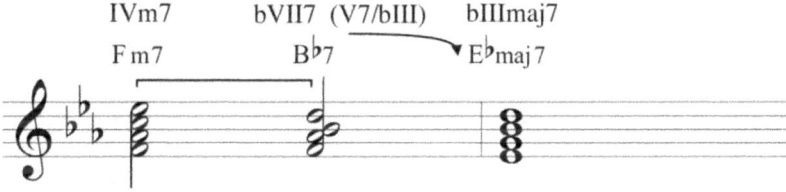

In this case we usually keep the diatonic analysis of the secondary dominant (bVII7) rather than V7/bIII.

Our corresponding chord for the II-V cadence will be Fm7, which is IVm7 and diatonic to the C natural minor scale.

## Secondary Dominant of the Fourth Degree (V7/IV):

The secondary dominant of the fourth degree in C minor will be the same chord as its parallel major tonality: C7. It has two different available resolutions: The IVm7, which comes from the natural and harmonic minor diatonic scale, and the IV7, which comes from the melodic minor scale.

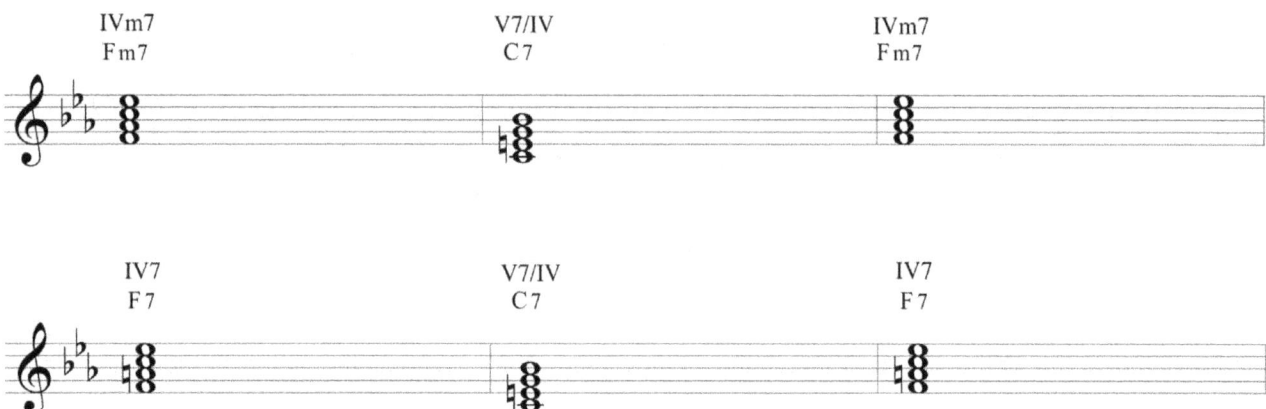

Corresponding II-V cadence:

In this case we can have a II-V cadence that can resolve either to Fm7 or to F7. The corresponding "II chord" is Gm7 and this is the Vm7 (Diatonic) of C natural minor:

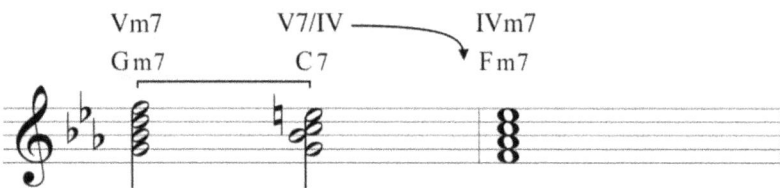

It is also very common to alter the Gm7 and convert it into a Gm7(b5) in order to tonicize the Fm7 due to the Db that is contained within the Gm7(b5). This is not a diatonic chord at all, but it is commonly used for a II-V cadence that resolves to the IVm7:

Observe that in this case the Gm7(b5) does not have an analysis because it's not diatonic.

The exact same thing can be applied when resolving to the IV7 chord (from C melodic minor):

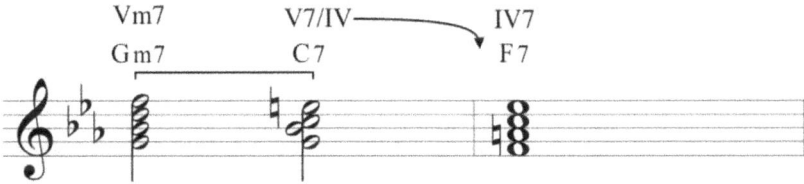

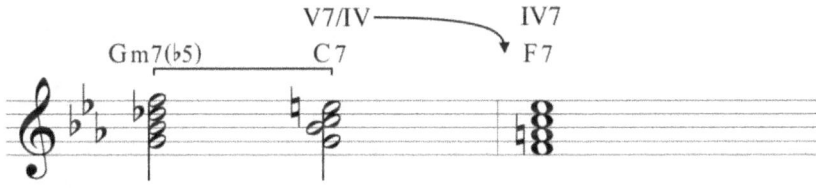

## Secondary Dominant of the Fifth Degree (V7/V):

The secondary dominant for the fifth degree in a minor scale will be the same as in the parallel major tonality: D7. This chord has two resolutions. The first one is a dominant minor chord, which comes from the natural minor scale, and the second one is a dominant seventh chord, which comes from the harmonic/melodic minor.

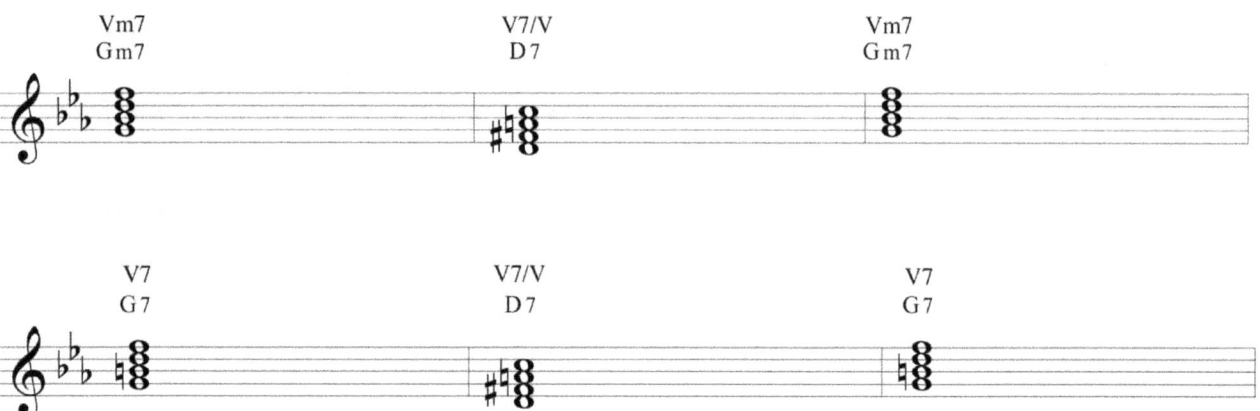

Corresponding II-V Cadence:

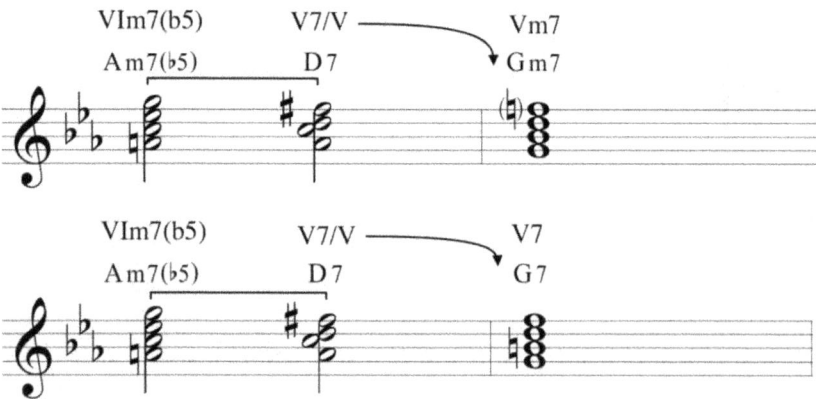

## Secondary Dominant of the Flat Sixth Degree (V7/bVII):

Observe that the VIm7(b5) from the melodic minor scale doesn't really have a secondary dominant because of its half-diminished quality. You could potentially say that E7 is the secondary dominant for Am7(b5) but inside the C minor tonality, this is a very strange resolution that almost never happens in common practice.

Corresponding II-V cadence:

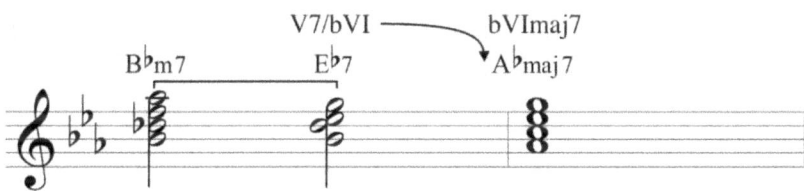

## Secondary Dominant of the Flat Seventh Degree (V7/bVII or IV7):

In the case of the natural minor scale, we get a secondary dominant for the bVII7 degree: F7, which ends up being a diatonic chord of C melodic minor (IV7).

Just like we did with the secondary dominant of the flat three degree, we keep the diatonic analysis (IV7).

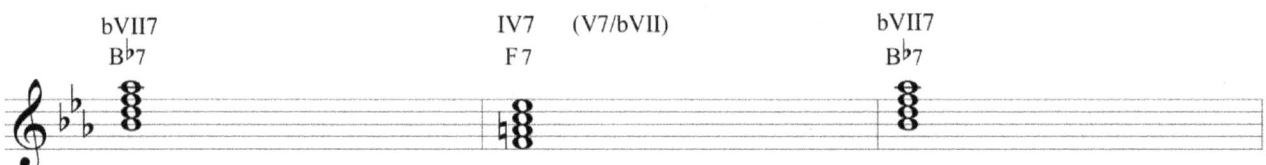

Corresponding II-V Cadence:

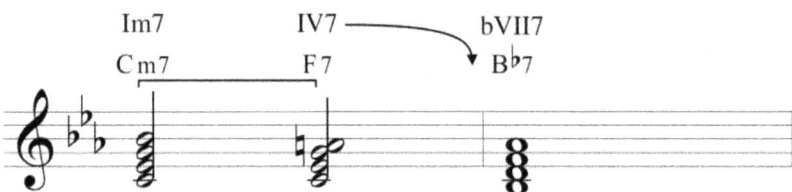

These are all the secondary dominants of a minor tonality (using C minor as an example)

Next, let's take a look at some minor tonality examples using all the concepts discussed in this chapter.

Page left blank to facilitate chart reading

120 | *Applications of Contemporary Harmony I*

## Example #1

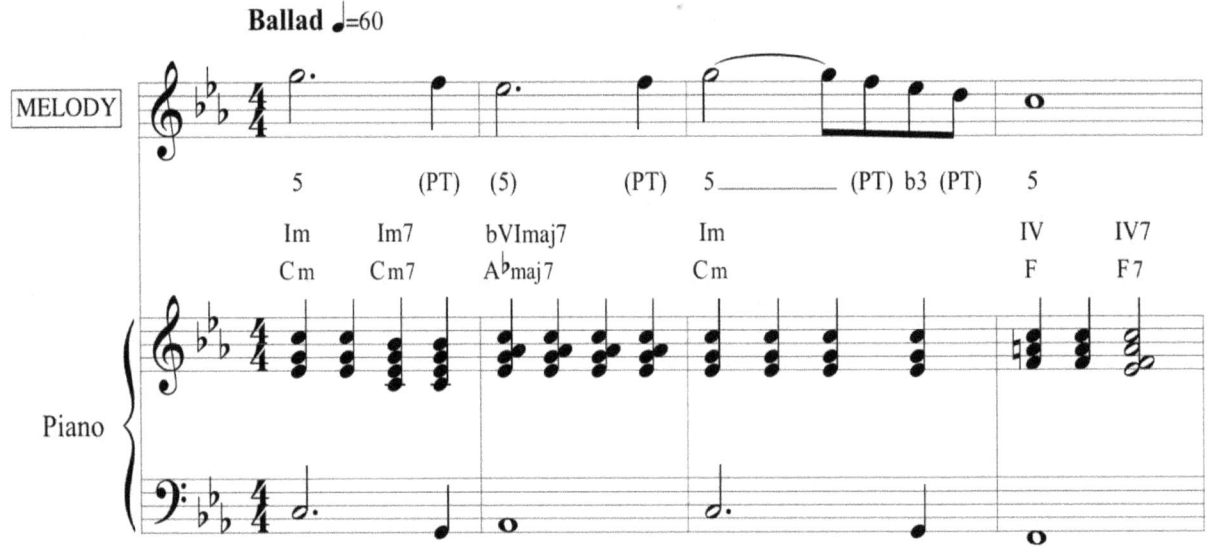

In the example above you can see a simple melody and harmonic progression in the key of C minor which uses chords from all of the minor scales that we've seen (natural, harmonic and melodic minor) and also some secondary dominants and II-V cadences.

# [5]
# Chord extensions 1: Introduction and Basic Application

## Diatonic Natural Tensions

SO FAR, we have studied all the diatonic functions in the major and minor tonalities, along with their corresponding secondary dominants. We have seen how all of these chords work together and how to use some of them for harmonization and reharmonization purposes. We have also talked about basic non-chord tones, which serve as efficient melodic devices to connect the chord tones. We have used these non-chord tones as unimportant notes (not sustained on a strong beat and usually acting as a sort of small bridge between one chord-tone and another). In this chapter we will introduce the concept of extended harmony, which is something that has been used extensively in contemporary music.

*Chord extensions* are thirds added above a regular seventh chord (major, minor, dominant, augmented or diminished), which provide the chord with a fuller, dense and more complex sound; they are also extremely useful melodic devices.

In most of the examples that we will study during this chapter, we will see chord extensions being used as important melody notes.

Chord extensions are also known as "harmonic tensions" or simply "tensions" and they originate from the scale that corresponds to the chord; in diatonic harmony, as we've seen on chapter 1, every scale degree has its own scale which is known as a mode. These scales contain the corresponding chord's chord tones as well as the diatonic non-chord tones which, when applied vertically, become the chord extensions.

We know that a seventh chord contains the scale degrees 1, 3 or b3, 5 or b5 and 7 or b7 and the rest scale degrees are non-chords: 2, 4 and 6 (Passing tones, neighbor tones, escape tones, suspensions, etc.) usually used as melodic devices and decorations executed on weak beats or upbeats. Now, we will use these notes as melodic and harmonic devices by analyzing them as chord extensions. Harmonically, these notes are built above the seventh of the chord; therefore they will be called 9, 11 and 13 rather than 2, 4 and 6.

*Natural tensions* are non-chord tones that are a diatonic step above each chord tone of the corresponding scale. The available natural tensions (for harmonic and melodic purposes) have to be a whole step above the chord tones.

It is very important to know that tensions that are a half step above a chord tone are altered tensions and they can **only** happen in dominant chords (with rare exceptions) since they need the tri-tone of the dominant in order to work.

Let's see how this applies in the diatonic chords in the key of C major.

We start with the Imaj7 chord, which will be Cmaj7 and then build the corresponding diatonic scale (mode), which in this case will be the Ionian mode (major scale):

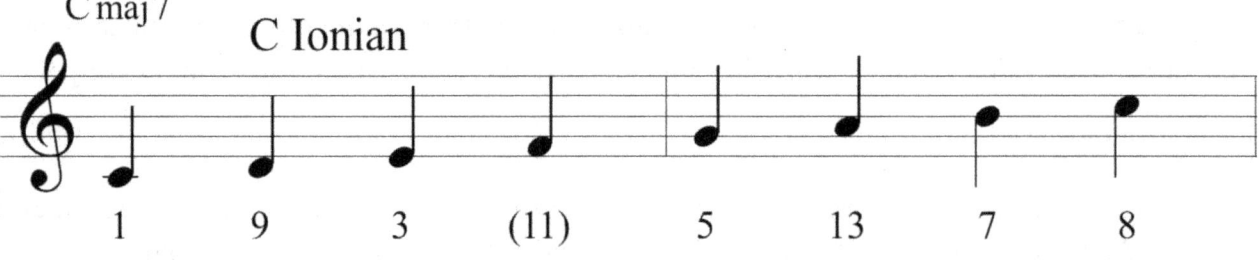

You can see how the 2nd, 4th and 6th degrees have been renamed to 9, 11 and 13. This is because in harmony theory, they come above the seventh, but they can be placed anywhere. Remember that in earlier chapters we've always analyzed these notes as non-chord tones, for which we used 2, 4 and 6, and they merely served as passing melodic devices; Now, we are analyzing them as harmonic extensions of the chords, which means that they can be used as part of the harmonization and as a strong melodic component rather than passing melodic devices (as we will see in the next examples). This basically means that melodically, we can use these available tensions with the same importance as the chord tones.

This is how these chord extensions would look like on top of the Cmaj7 chord:

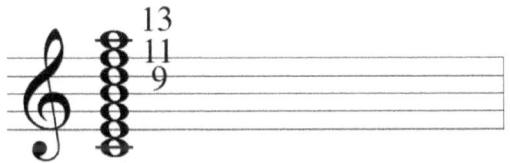

As we can see in the previous diagram of the C major scale, the 11th is in parenthesis, which means that it only serves as a passing tone (non-chord tone) and not as a sustained tension since it is a half-step above a chord tone (the third) and the natural tensions need to be a whole step above.

Keep in mind that as a general rule, the 11th degree is an avoid note in any major or dominant chord, so for this chord, only the 9th and 13th will be diatonically available.

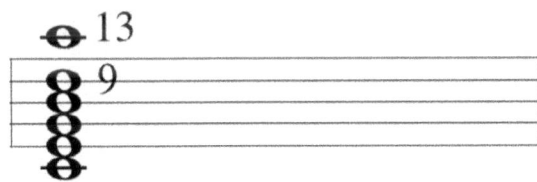

In this case the 11th can also be altered so that it becomes a whole step above the third rather than a half step. This is how all the available tensions would look like for Cmaj7:

Cmaj7(9,#11.13)

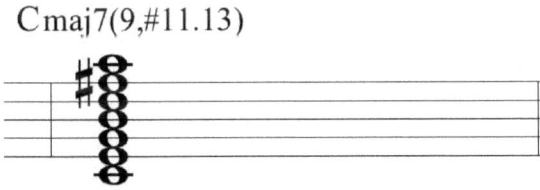

As you can see, all the available tensions together form a D triad over the Cmaj7.

126 | *Applications of Contemporary Harmony I*

Let's continue with all the diatonic chords in the key of C major:

-Dm7 (IIm7)

Corresponding scale (mode):

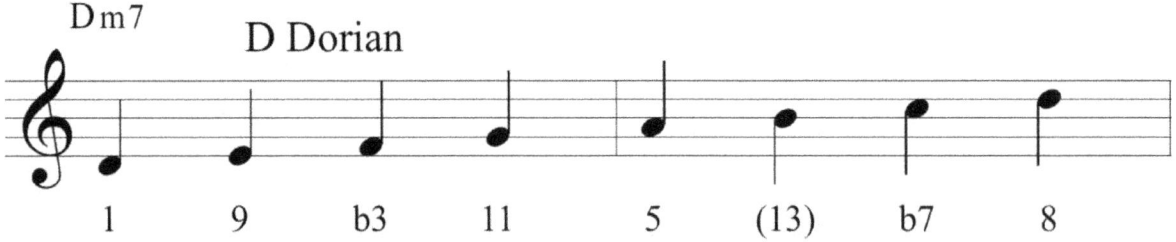

Corresponding chord extensions:

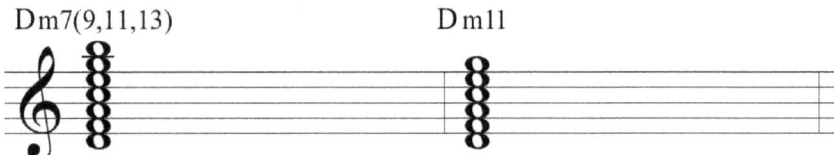

In this case all the corresponding diatonic tensions are a whole step above the chord tones, so potentially they could all be used. Keep in mind that within a II-V cadence, the $13^{th}$ of the II chord is the same note as the third of the V chord; therefore it's not recommended to use it since it will anticipate the function of the V chord.

- Em7 (IIIm7)

Corresponding scale (mode):

Corresponding chord extensions:

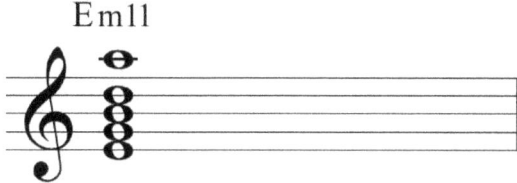

In this case we can see a b9 (from the Phrygian scale), which is a half-step above a chord tone (the root) so it will be an unavailable tension. The same happens with the b13. So the only available tension for the IIIm7 will be the 11th, which in this case will be the note A.

For this chord, we can alter the b9 in order to get a natural 9th so that we can use it as an available tension (just like we did with the 11th in the Cmaj7 chord):

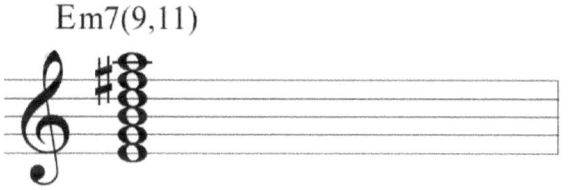

- Fmaj7 (IVmaj7)

Corresponding scale (mode):

The Lydian scale is very special in the sense that it doesn't have any avoid notes; this is to say that all of the scale notes can be used as important melodic and harmonic devices. As you can see, all of the non-chord tones are a whole step above a chord tone.

Corresponding chord extensions:

Fmaj7(9,#11,13)

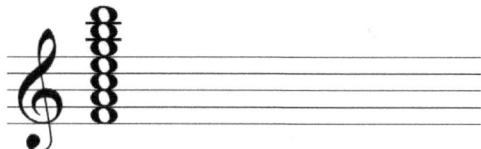

- G7 (V7)

Corresponding scale (mode):

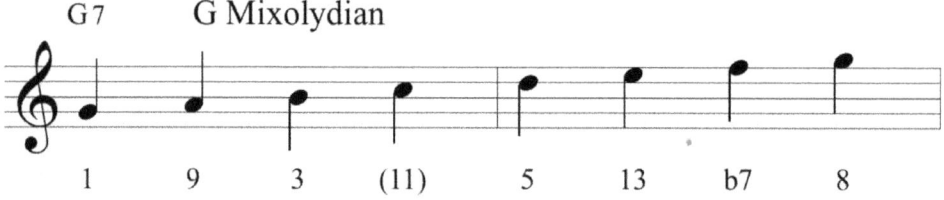

Corresponding chord extensions:

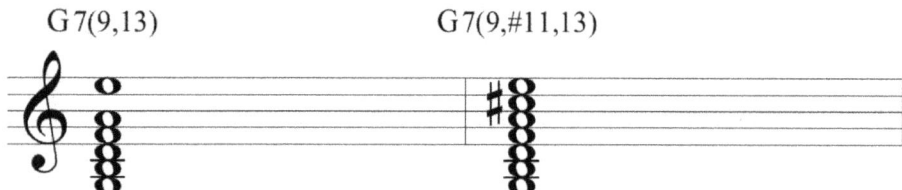

Notice how for harmonic purposes, the 11th has been altered to a #11 (Just like we did for Cmaj7). This can be done for any Major or Dominant chord to avoid the natural 11th. (It is important to keep in mind when composing, which altering the 11th to a #11th will provide the chord with a Lydian sonority.)

- Am7 (VIm7)

Corresponding scale (mode):

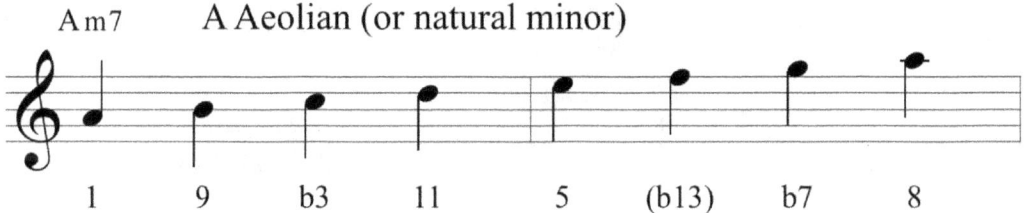

Corresponding chord extensions:

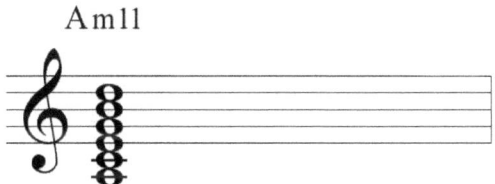

For this chord, it is possible to use the F# as a 13$^{th}$ but it is not very common.

- Bm7(b5)

Corresponding scale (mode):

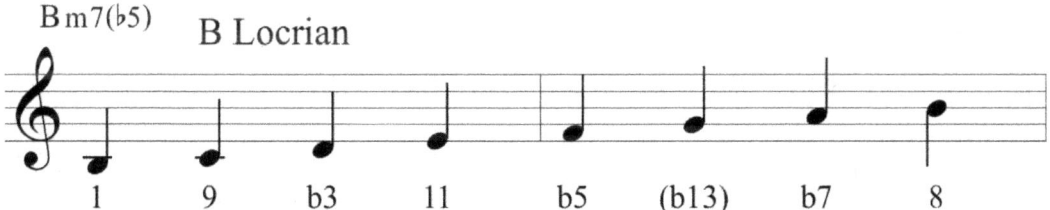

Corresponding chord extensions:

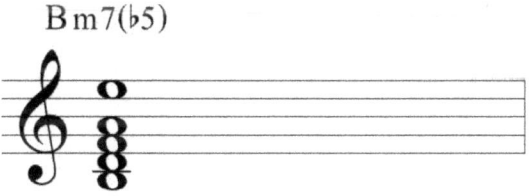

## Table of Natural Harmonic Tensions in C major:

| Diatonic Chord Name | Diatonic Chord Function | Available Tensions (9, 11, 13?) | Available Tensions (corresponding notes) |
|---|---|---|---|
| Cmaj7 | Imaj7 | 9, (#11) and 13 | D, F#, A |
| Dm7 | IIm7 | 9 and 11. (sometimes 13) | E, G. (Sometimes B) |
| Em7 | IIIm7 | (9) and 11 | (F#) and A |
| Fmaj7 | IVmaj7 | 9, #11 and 13 | G, B and D |
| G7 | V7 | 9, (#11) and 13 | A, (C#) and E |
| Am7 | VIm7 | 9, 11. (Sometimes 13) | B, D. (Sometimes F#) |
| Bm7(b5) | VIIm7(b5) | 11 | E |

This table shows all of the available tensions but these chords can have any combination of these tensions:

Different Combinations (Chord Symbols that specify tensions):

- Imaj7: Cmaj7, Cmaj9, Cmaj7(9,13), Cmaj7 (#11), Cmaj7(9,#11,13)

C(add9) is also a very common chord in popular music. This means that the chord will only have the ninth as a harmonic tension without the seventh.

- IIm7: Dm7, Dm9, Dm11

- IIIm7: Em7, Em9, Em11

- IVmaj7: Fmaj7, Fmaj9, Fmaj7(9,13), Fmaj7(#11), Fmaj7(9,#11,13)

- V7: G7, G9, G7(9,13), G7(#11), G7(9,#11,13)

- VIm7: Am7, Am9, Am11

- VIIm7(b5): Bm7(b5)

*Applications of Contemporary Harmony I* | 131

In contemporary music, it is very common to add some tensions to the chords even when they are not specified in the chord symbol; this is done to provide a richer and more sophisticated color to the harmony and it will usually be done by proficient guitarists and pianists.

## Introduction to Diatonic chord scale theory

A *chord scale* is a set of notes that represent the sound quality of a chord and its function in relation to a given tonality. In diatonic harmony, chord scales are basically the seven modes that we know (Ionian, Dorian, Phrygian, Lydian, Mixolydian, Aeolian and Locrian) and they contain all the available tensions of their corresponding chord (Imaj7, IIm7, IIIm7, IVmaj7, V7, VIm7, VIIm7(b5)).

The chord scale theory is what makes us understand where all the possible harmonic extensions come from, how to manipulate them to generate an extensive possibility of sound and, just like the name implies, how to create harmonic and melodic tension that will provide a more expressive character to the music. This section will serve as an introduction to this extensive theory of harmonic extensions.

### Identifying a chord scale:

In order to identify a chord scale, we simply need to write the chord-tones of the desired chord and then complete the missing scale notes with notes that are diatonic to the corresponding tonality.

For example: If we are in the key of C major and we are trying to identify the chord scale for Fmaj7, we start by writing down the chord-tones and leaving an empty space for every other scale note:

Then we simply complete the empty spaces with diatonic notes from C major in order to get the chord scale for Fmaj7:

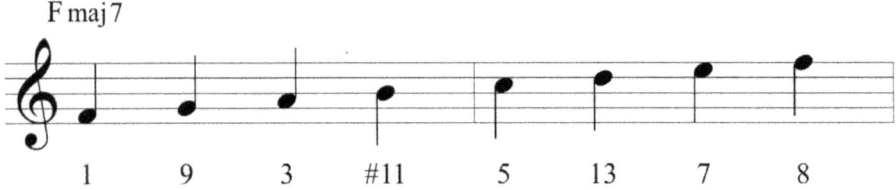

As a consequence, we get an F Lydian scale with 3 available tensions (9, #11 and 13).

Remember that the Lydian scale is very special since *all* the non-chord tones are available tensions (not just one or two like in other diatonic scales)

## CHORD EXTENSIONS IN SECONDARY DOMINANTS

So with this idea in mind, let's construct the basic chord scale for each of the secondary dominants in C major and see how we get different combinations of tensions depending on the function of the chord.

Keep in mind, that the corresponding chord extensions for each of these secondary dominants come from a diatonic source; nothing will be changed. Remember that since we are now talking about dominants, we don't only have natural tensions but we can also have altered tensions.

All the tensions in the following images are a diatonic result of C major. You will see that the dominants that resolve to minor degrees will contain altered tensions and the ones that resolve to major degrees will contain natural tensions.

These are the corresponding chord scales for each of the secondary dominants in C major:

All the secondary dominants will contain a specific type of Mixolydian scale, which will determine a set of available tensions for each individual chord. There are three different types of Mixolydian scales that we will see while analyzing secondary dominant chord scales. We will analyze them as we go through them:

## V7 (Primary Dominant)

This is the primary dominant of the tonality and it will form a Mixolydian scale.

Available Tensions: 9$^{th}$ and 13$^{th}$ (with the possibility of altering the natural 11$^{th}$ into a #11$^{th}$)

## V7/II

The five seven of two contains a natural 9$^{th}$ and a flat 13$^{th}$ as a diatonic result. This scale is known as mixolydian b13$^{th}$.

## V7/III

The five seven (V7) of the third degree contains a flat 9$^{th}$ and a flat 13$^{th}$.

To avoid the interval of an augmented second between the b9$^{th}$ and the third, we add another note, the #9 (which will be a minor third above the root) and this will become an available tension. As a general rule, both altered 9ths (b9 and #9) will always be available together; <u>you should never combine a natural 9$^{th}$ with an altered 9$^{th}$</u>.

The resulting chord scale for this chord will be the Mixolydian (b9, #9, b13), which will end up being an 8 note scale:

134 | *Applications of Contemporary Harmony I*

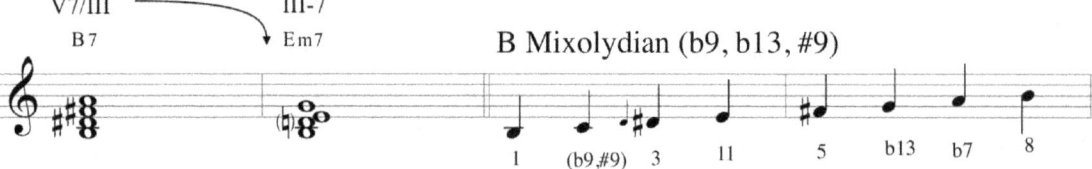

## V7/IV

This dominant resolves to the sub-dominant degree, which is major. When constructing the chord scale for this chord we end up with a Mixolydian (the same scale type used for the V7 chord)

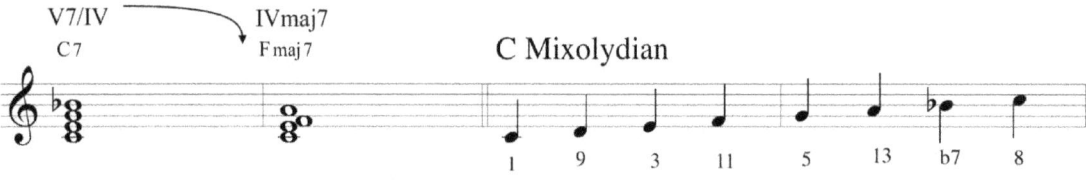

## V7/V

This is the only secondary dominant that will resolve to another dominant (the primary dominant) unless the resolution is used as a triad (G).

As you can see, the same result will be obtained as the one in V7/IV.

Finally, we have the chord scale for the V7/VI, which resolves to a minor chord.

In this case, when applying the diatonic chord scale theory, we will get the same type of scale that we got for the V7/III: Mixolydian (b9,#9,b13)

## V7/VI

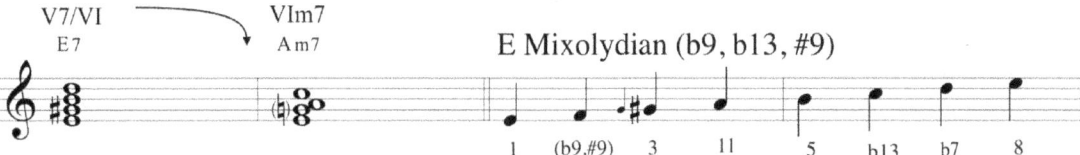

As you can see from the previous explanations, it is possible to generalize the fact that the dominants that resolve to major chords contain natural available tensions and the dominants that resolve to minor chords contain altered available tensions.

This happens as a diatonic result with the non-chord tones that belong to the current key. If we were in the key of C minor, then all the scales for the secondary dominants would follow the corresponding key signature of C minor (same as Eb major). This would give us the same three Mixolydian scales that we've seen so far, but placed on different chords or chords with a different functionality; For example, V7 in C major results in a G Mixolydian scale but that same function in C minor results in a G Mixolydian (b9, b13, #9):

### V7 in C minor (G7)

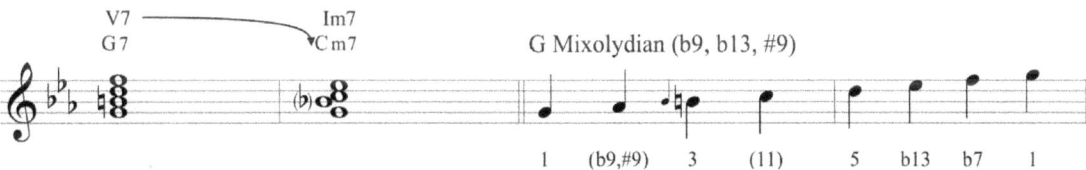

Most chord extensions can be altered or naturalized from their original state. (Whatever the chord scale indicates) This is a more advanced topic that will be discussed thoroughly in the next book, *"Applications of Contemporary Harmony II"*.

In the following example, we can see a 16-bar jazz tune where some tensions have been used as important melodic devices. Notice that now we are not analyzing the non-chord tones as we did before (PT, NT, ET, Sus, etc.), but we are using the name of the tension in relationship to the chord.

All the chords in this example show the exact tensions that were used in the melody; this is not necessary, unless the tension that will be used is altered from its corresponding chord scale, which is not the case (except for the A7b9).

In Jazz harmonic vocabulary, it is not necessary to specify every tension used in the melody since most well trained jazz pianists or guitarists will know what tensions to add in the voicings depending on the context. It is important tough, to specify the tensions in the chord symbols if you want to make sure that that specific note will be included in the voicing.

Let's take a look at the following example:

This example uses a typical swing vocabulary melodically and harmonically. We can see how certain notes that are anticipated to the next measure, are analyzed as being part of the next chord rather than being part of the chord in which it starts (E.g.: The melody note A between measure 3 and 4). This is something very typical in Jazz music but you can also see it in other styles (E.g.: In classical music you could have that note untied and it would be analyzed as anticipation)

Going back to this example, let's analyze the chord scales and tensions that apply:

| Chords (in order of appearance) | Function | Corresponding Chord Scale | Available Tensions | Available Tensions (Name of the note/s) | Tension/s used in the melody (per chord) | Tension/s used in the melody (Name of the note/s) |
|---|---|---|---|---|---|---|
| Cmaj9 | Imaj7 | C Ionian | 9, (#11), 13 | D, (F#), A | 9 | D |
| G7sus4 | V7sus4 | G Mixolydian | 9, (3), 13 | (A, B, E) | No tensions used | |
| Cmaj9 | Imaj7 | C Ionian | 9, (#11), 13 | D, (F#), A | 9, 13 | D, A |
| Gm9 | | G Dorian | 9, 11 | A, C | 9 | A |
| C7(9,13) | V7/IV | C Mixolydian | 9, 13 | D, A | 9, 13 | D, A |
| Fmaj9 | IVmaj7 | F Lydian | 9, #11, 13 | G, B, D | 9 | G |
| Em7 | IIIm7 | E Phrygian | 11 | A | | |
| A7(b9) | V7/II | A Mixolydian (b13) | b9, b13 | Bb, F | b9 | Bb |
| D9 | V7/V | D Mixolydian | 9, 13 | E, B | 9 | E |
| G9 | V7 | G Mixolydian | 9, 13 | A, E | 9 | A |
| Cmaj9 | Imaj7 | C Ionian | 9, (#11), 13 | D, F#, A | 9 | D |
| G7sus4 | V7 | G Mixolydian | 9, 13 | A, E | No tensions used | |
| Cmaj9 | Imaj7 | C Ionian | 9, (#11), 13 | D, (F#), A | 9 | D |
| Bm7(b5) | VIIm7(b5) | B Locrian | 13 | E | No tensions used | |
| E7(b9) | V7/VI | E Mixolydian (b9, b13, #9) | b9, #9, b13 | F, G, C | b9, b13 | F, C |
| Am9 | VIm7 | Aeolian | 9, 11 | B, D | 9 | 9 |
| D13 | V7/V | D Mixolydian | 9, 13 | E, B | 13 | B |
| Dm9 | IIm7 | D Dorian | 9, 11 | E, G | 9 | E |
| G13 | V7 | G Mixolydian | 9, 13 | A, E | 13 | E |
| Cmaj9 | Imaj7 | C Ionian | 9, (#11), 13 | D, (F#), A | 9 | D |

It is important to mention at this point that Sus chords (E.g.: G7sus4) use the same scale as the regular dominant chord (G7). The only difference is that for the Sus chord, the third of the chord will be a non-chord tone (as opposed to the natural 11th like in the regular dominant) but they both have the same harmonic function. This means that the third can actually become a natural tension (just like explained on the table above).

Also notice that for some chords in this progression certain tensions that are not necessarily in the melody have been specified (this is the case of the C7(9,13) where only the 13th is being used); this means that the 9th will serve as a harmonic device for the voicing that will harmonize that melody). It is important to know that tensions that are above a 9th (11th and 13th), especially in Jazz music, usually already contain the 9th as part of their structure for a fuller sound. This means that if we see a chord like D13, it will most likely contain the 9th (E) and the specified 13th (B) as part of the voicing.

# [6] Harmonization and Reharmonization 2

IN THIS CHAPTER, we will learn how to apply all the concepts discussed so far. We will start with some reharmonization examples first, and then we will do a complete walk through of how to harmonize a complete tune on an AABA form.

## REHARMONIZATION USING ALL THE TOPICS FROM THIS BOOK

Harmonization and reharmonization are almost the same thing in the sense that in order to harmonize a melody from scratch, you need to think about many possible options that would fit best on a given context, this process is the same for reharmonizing. In other words, in order to generate an efficient harmonic progression, you need to be able to think on chord variations and possibilities.

140 | *Applications of Contemporary Harmony I*

Let's start with a very simple example, the song "Twinkle, Twinkle" that we used on chapter 2, but this time on Bb Major:

This is the song on its most basic form with a very simple harmonic language based on Tonic, Sub-Dominant and Dominant functions. Now I will show you several ways in which you can reharmonize this song with all of the harmonic theory we have learnt so far.

By now, you should be very familiar with the 4 bar phrases, 8 measure sections, 12 bar songs, 16 bar songs and 32 bar songs (all coming from an even construction of phrases). So let's consider this while working on this song. This version of *Twinkle, Twinkle* is constructed as a 12 bar song, which can be sub-divided into 3 distinctive sections: Section A (first 4 measures), section B (following 4 measures) and back to section A (last 4 measures).

Let's start by enhancing the color of the chords by adding sevenths and also adding and/or replacing chords that belong to the same functional group (Tonic, Sub-Dominant or Dominant).

# REHARMONIZATION 1 (Diatonic Chords)

This reharmonization provides a fuller sound and takes us away from that triadic sound of the original version. We can also see how at certain moments the harmonic rhythm has increased. For example, in measure 1 a chord from the same family has been added in order to create more movement and to add color to the progression.

## REHARMONIZATION 2 (Diatonic chords, chord extensions and acceleration of harmonic rhythm)

Now, let's add some natural chord extensions to some of these chords to make the progression "jazzier", and let's also try to turn some of the melody notes into chord extensions.

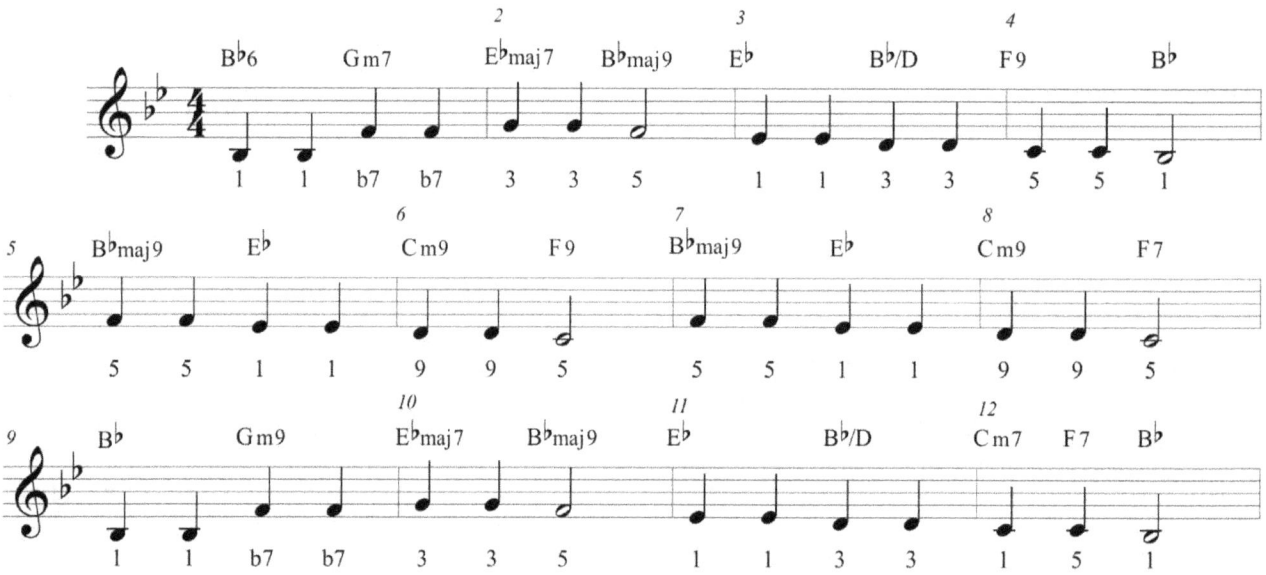

Notice how on bar 6 the Bb chord changed to a Cm7 chord making the melody note D the 9th. This provides a thicker color to the melody. Especially if all the other melody notes are chord tones, just like on this example. Also see how the harmonic rhythm increased on measure 12 (Always remember that accelerating the harmonic rhythm is a great reharmonization device, especially for endings!)

# REHARMONIZATION 3 (Diatonic chords, chord extensions, secondary dominants, acceleration of harmonic rhythm) – Includes Analysis:

Now let's include some secondary dominants to the harmonic progression:

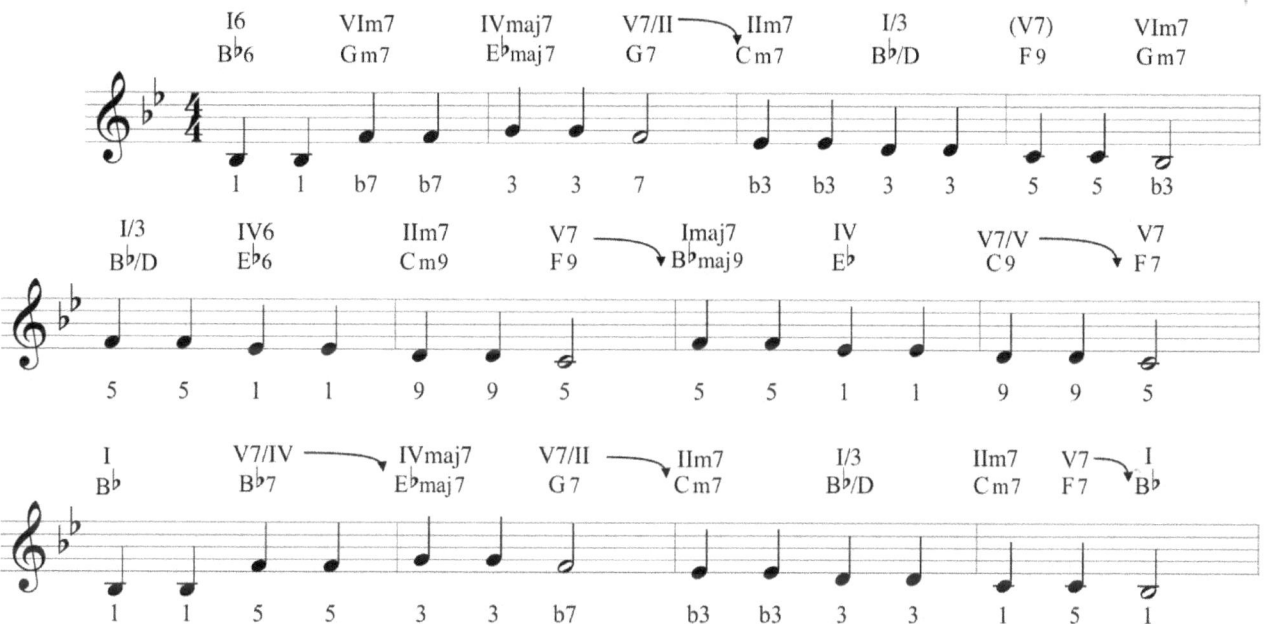

Once we start including secondary dominants, we finally get away from that complete diatonic sound and we start getting chromatic notes on the inner voices. The secondary dominants also allow the progression to have more movement and tonicizing to other diatonic degrees (E.g.: the G7 resolving to Cm7 from measure 2 to measure 3, or the C9 resolving to F7 on measure 8)

# REHARMONIZATION 4 (DIATONIC CHORDS, CHORD EXTENSIONS, SECONDARY DOMINANTS, II-V CADENCES, ACCELERATION OF HARMONIC RHYTHM)

Now, let's add II-V cadences to some of the secondary dominants in this progression:

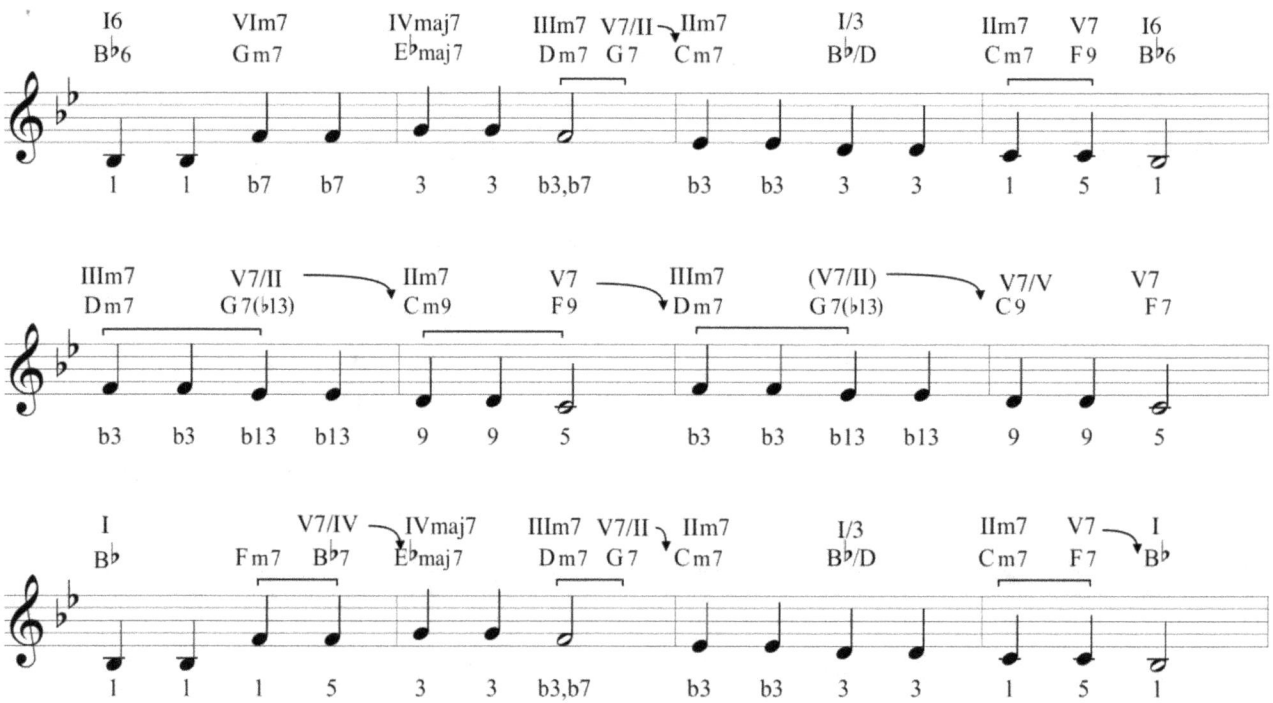

The addition of the II-V cadences of the secondary dominants provide a much fuller chord progression and a much more interesting bass movement. Notice how most of the II-V cadences happen on an accelerated harmonic rhythm (one chord per beat). (E.g.: Measure 2, 4, 9, 10 and 12). The II-V cadence also makes the listener believe there is a slight shift of harmonic direction (just like the II-V of the IVmaj7 degree on measure 9 going to measure 10) or even a possibility of modulating to another diatonic degree, although the chords that follow clearly notate that we are still on the same key and we've only moved around diatonic degrees with the use of II-V cadences.

# REHARMONIZATION 5 (CHANGING THE HARMONIC DIRECTION OF THE PROGRESSION)

Another way of reharmonizing a given progression is by changing the intension of the song completely. This can be done by either implying another tonality (for example the relative minor tonality) or by reharmonizing with more complex chords or non-functional harmony.

Let's try reharmonizing this melody by implying the key of the relative minor, which would be G minor:

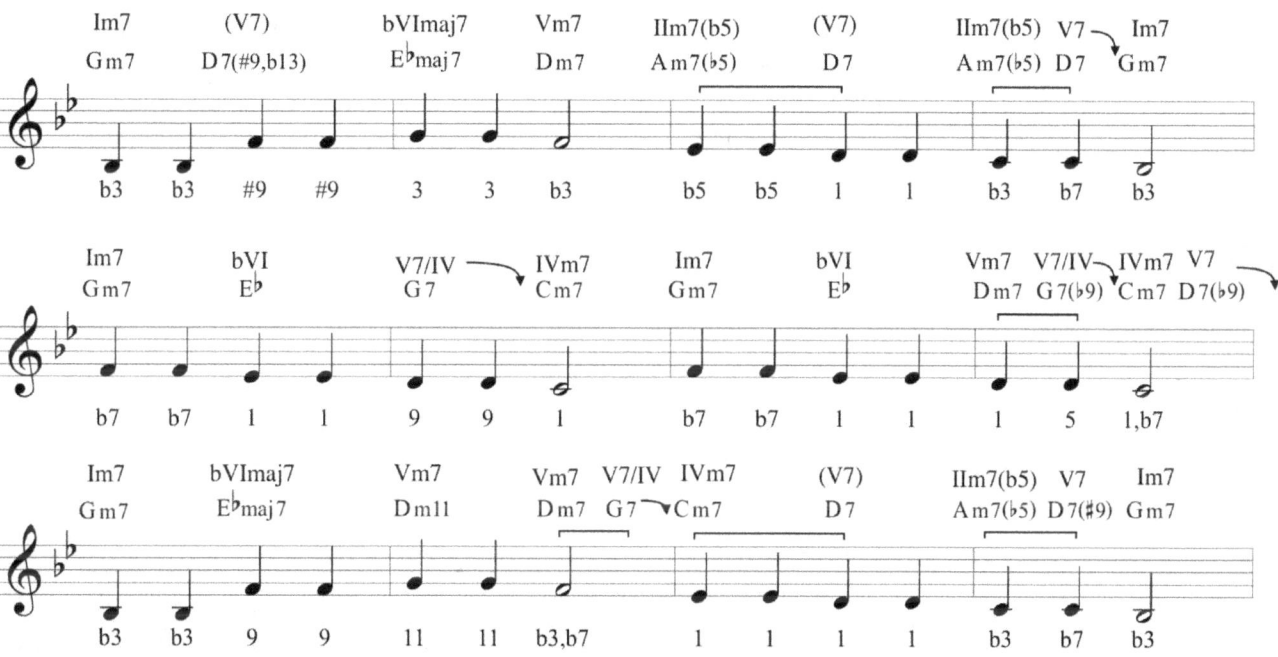

This is a great way of reharmonizing by re-enforcing a related key to the harmonic progression. I say *related key*, because you wouldn't be able to harmonize this melody with the diatonic chords of B major (half a step away) since you would have to alter all the notes accordingly. However, you could easily re-harmonize this in G minor (just like in the example), in F major (up a fifth), in Eb major (down a fifth) or in any other key close enough to Bb in the circle of fifths.

Let's do another reharmonization for an extract of the Christmas song *"Jingle Bells"*

146 | *Applications of Contemporary Harmony I*

This is the song with its basic harmonic progression in G major:

# Jingle Bells

As you can see in the image above, the basic harmonic progression of Jingle Bells is built on the three main functions of a tonality (Tonic, Sub-Dominant and Dominant functions). Let's do a couple more reharmonizations using some of the concepts discussed on this book.

# REHARMONIZATION 1 (DIATONIC CHORD SUBSTITUTIONS, ADDITION OF SEVENTH CHORDS, CHORD EXTENSIONS):

# REHARMONIZATION 2 (Diatonic chord substitutions, addition of seventh chords, chord extensions, secondary dominants, II-V cadences):

NOTE: (About measure 14)

It is highly common, especially in Jazz, to make the "II" of the "II - V" cadence a half-diminished chord (in this case Bm7b5) in order to darken the cadence and make it sound more minor. This is specifically common with the II – V cadence for the second degree since we are resolving to a minor chord (IIm7), but we have a IIIm7 as a diatonic result for this cadence. As we've already seen, dominants that resolve to minor chords are usually accompanied with a m7(b5) chord rather than a m7 chord (just like the II – V cadence for the IIIm7 degree and the VIm7 degree). So, by doing this, you provide a darker sound that will enhance the feeling of resolving to a minor chord (IIm7). The Bm7(b5) is not analyzed on its own since it is not diatonic to G major. Also notice how the b5 of the Bm7(b5) becomes the b9 of the E7(b9).

## REHARMONIZATION 2 WITH GUIDE TONES

Now, let's use the last example (Reharmonization 2) and generate some guide tones that will help enhance the progression and will serve as an effective counterpoint to the melody:

The guide tones in the previous image are constructed by the thirds and sevenths of the chords except on measure 9 where we can see a 1$^{st}$ and 5$^{th}$ as one of the two guide tones; this is because the third is already on the melody.

Also notice how on measure 1 and 2 the top guide tone works as a descending counter line to the melody. This is an efficient way of using guide tones; not just having them sustain as 3rds and seventh, but try to work out a melodic line that could easily serve as a counterpoint to the melody.

## Harmonization Process

### How to designate a chord progression to a given song/tune.

All the process applied to the next example can be used in the same way when reharmonizing (again, remember that harmonization and reharmonization are really the same process, the only difference being that one generates harmony and the other one reconstructs it over an existing progression), but the methods and concepts are the same!.

[For this section you will need to reference the following lead sheet constantly, so have it in hand.]

The following example is a jazz waltz. Let's take a look at the melody and form in order to determine our harmonic cadences and start the harmonization process.

Page left blank to facilitate chart reading

# Reharm Waltz

Lorenzo Ferrero

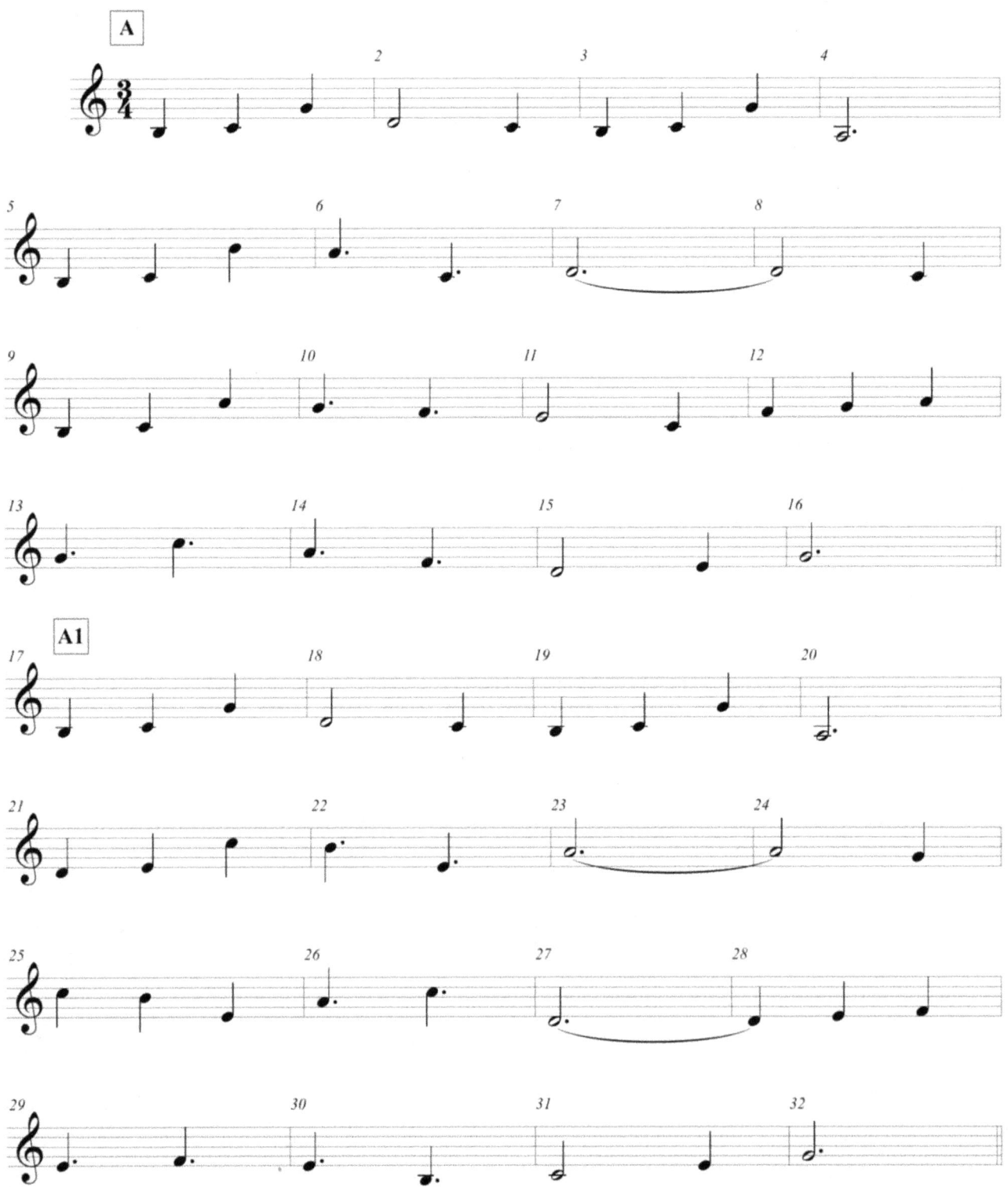

## Applications of Contemporary Harmony I

This tune is in the typical AABA form, but with a slightly unusual amount of measures. The three A sections (the first two and the last one) are 16 bars each and the B section is extended to 24 bars. The A sections (A, A1 and A2) are slightly different from each other but they are all constructed uniquely by the C major diatonic scale. The B section contains certain chromatic notes that will suggest a specific secondary dominant or will be simply a chromatic approach (like the D# on measure 33).

It is very common for students to try to start using as many chords as possible when they start harmonizing or reharmonizing in order to feel that they are applying everything that they know; this is a mistake. The best way to start the harmonization process is to make a simple plan that determines the direction of your progression. Considering that the melody of the A section is completely diatonic, it would be best to start with diatonic harmonization and by identifying the possible cadences at the end of the phrases and in between them.

Remember that sophisticated chords have a much bigger effect when NOT used that often; if you start using more complex chords too often you will most likely overwhelm the listener and the chord(s) will lose its/their effect completely. It's like putting too much sugar on a cake.

Let's start by harmonizing the sections independently (make sure that you have the previous image for this since we will be referencing it constantly measure by measure):

## A Section (Mainly diatonic harmonization):

If we take a look at the first 4 measures, we can see that the melody is implying a tonic function all the way through (as the simplest version) but we could say that measure 2 and 4 could easily imply a sub-dominant function chord (IVmaj7 or IIm7).

For this harmonization, I will keep the tonic function chord (Imaj7) for the first two measures so that we can keep the harmonic beat slow at the beginning. Measure 4 is a perfect spot to change function (in order to go right back to tonic function on measure 5) so I will make it a IVmaj7 (Fmaj7) which will go perfectly with the A in the melody. Measure 3 will stay on the tonic function but I will add the third in the bass (E) in order to lead chromatically to the Fmaj7 chord. Measure 5 and 6 clearly imply the tonic function so we could actually harmonize these two measures with Imaj7 (Cmaj7), IIm7 (Em7) or VIm7 (Am7). Since the melody in measure 5 contains the note C, Em7 won't be a good option because it is an avoid note. Considering that I harmonized measure 1 and 2 with only one chord, I will slightly accelerate the harmonic beat by harmonizing measure 5 with Imaj7 (Cmaj7) and measure 6 with VIm7 (Am7). Furthermore, we can see that measure 7 and 8 is a good spot for a cadence in order to go back to the tonic function on measure 9 (which is almost the same as measure 1), so I will add a IIm7 (Dm7) in measure 7 and a V7 (G7) in measure 8.

The next 4 measures (9 to 12) are very similar to the first 4 measures of the tune in the sense that they also imply the tonic function (measures 9 and 11) and the sub-dominant function (measures 10 and 12). Therefore, I will keep the Imaj7 (Cmaj7) for measures 9 and 11 and put a IV chord (F) on measure 12. (Notice that I'm avoiding the major seventh because it will clash with the F in the melody, which is a semitone apart from E)

On measure 10, I decided to put a V7sus4 chord (which belongs to the dominant function) instead of harmonizing it with another sub-dominant chord. This is simply for variation and root movement. Finally, we have the last 4 measures of section A (from 13 to 16), which is a great opportunity to think on an efficient cadence in order to go back to the tonic function on section A2 (measure 17). The best way to do this is to try to include a harmonic turnaround and accelerate the harmonic beat. In a 3/4 beat, there are two ways to include more than one chord per measure. One is to fit the first chord in the first 2 beats and the second chord on the third beat. The other way would be to put each chord on a dotted quarter note so that they last the same amount of time. In this case, measures 13 and 14 contain two dotted quarter notes each in the melody, so it would be of great intensity to harmonize each of the dotted quarter notes with a different chord.

In order to do this, let's first harmonize measures 15 and 16 so that we may know how this section will finish. Since we have to go back to the tonic function on measure 17, a simple solution would be to make measure 15 a IIm7 (Dm7) and measure 16 a V7 (G7) which is pretty much what the melody implies.

Finally, I decided to put a II-V cadence for the second degree on measure 13 (Em7 – A7) which will resolve to Dm7 on measure 14, and then go right back to the A7 chord on the second half of that measure in order to efficiently resolve to the Dm7 on measure 15.

Notice how some chords are spelled with specific tensions depending on what is on the melody. Also, on measure 13, I made the melody note C a tension of a non-diatonic chord (A7) and in measure 14, I made the melody note F (diatonic to C major) a tension of a non-diatonic chord (A7), which provides a much richer sound than the one of a regular chord-tone.

Additionally, the V7/II (A7) has a Mixolydian b13 scale as a diatonic result, but it is very common to also alter the natural $9^{th}$ and make the scale a Mixolydian (b9, b13, #9) – just like the V7/III and the V7/VI since it's a chord that will resolve to a minor chord (IIm7). This was done on measure 13 where I made the C the #9 of A7.

The concept of altering or naturalizing tensions will be discussed extensively on "Applications of Contemporary Harmony II".

This is how it looks like so far:

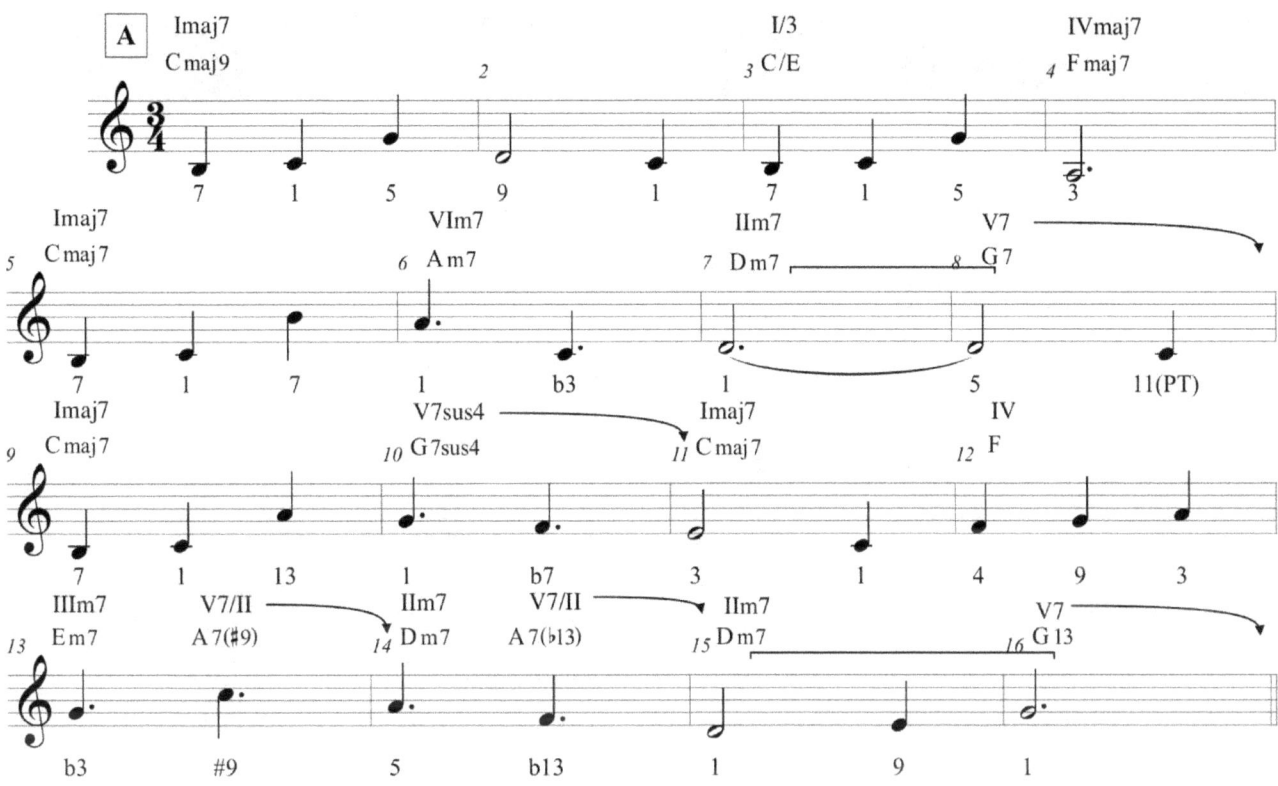

There are lots of harmonization and reharmonization options for this melody; I'm simply showing an easy approach to get you started on the concept of coloring a melody by the understanding of functional harmony (only considering the concepts discussed on this book). In "Applications of Contemporary Harmony II" we will do the same process but exploring a much bigger pallet of chords and functions.

The following table displays a measure-by-measure breakdown of this A section. This includes chord, function, chord scale, available tensions and tensions used.

| Measure # | Chord | Function | Chord-Scale | Available Natural Tensions | Tensions Used on Melody |
|---|---|---|---|---|---|
| 1 - 2 | Cmaj9 | Imaj7 | C Ionian or C Lydian | 9, (#11), 13 | 9 |
| 3 | C/E | I/3 | C Ionian or C Lydian | 9, (#11), 13 | |
| 4 | Fmaj7 | IVmaj7 | F Lydian | 9, #11, 13 | |
| 5 | Cmaj7 | Imaj7 | C Ionian or C Lydian | 9, (#11), 13 | |
| 6 | Am7 | VIm7 | A Aeolian | 9, 11 | |
| 7 | Dm7 | IIm7 | D Dorian | 9, 11, (13) | |
| 8 | G7 | V7 | G Mixolydian | 9, (#11), 13 | |
| 9 | Cmaj7 | Imaj7 | C Ionian or C Lydian | 9, (#11), 13 | 13 |
| 10 | G7sus4 | V7sus4 | G Mixolydian (Avoid 3) | 9, 10, 13 | |
| 11 | Cmaj7 | Ima7 | C Ionian or C Lydian | 9, (#11), 13 | |
| 12 | F | IV | F Lydian | 9, #11, 13 | 9 |
| 13 | -Em7<br>-A7(#9) | -IIIm7<br>-V7/II | -E Phrygian (or E Dorian)<br>-A Mixolydian b9,b13,#9 | -IIIm7= 9, 11<br>*-V7/II= b9,b13, #9 | -V7/II= #9 |
| 14 | -Dm7<br>-A7(b13) | -IIm7<br>-V7/II | -D Dorian<br>-A Mixolydian b13 | -IIm7=9, 11, (13)<br>*-V7/II= b9, b13, #9 | -V7/II= b13 |
| 15 | Dm7 | IIm7 | D Dorian | 9, 11, (13) | 9 |
| 16 | G13 | V7 | G Mixolydian | 9, (#11), 13 | |

Remember that all the chord extensions displayed on the table above are the consequence of their relationship with the home key (in this case C major); also remember that tensions in parenthesis are optional tensions that could also be placed over those chords.

The only chord that contains tensions that have been altered in this progression is the A7 (V7/II) on measure 13 and 14. Normally that chord will contain a Mixolydian b13 scale (with a natural 9), but in this case the 9th has been altered too. This is a very common thing to do for this specific function. The reason for that is because it is a Dominant that resolves to a minor chord (IIm7) and altering the 9th enhances that minor sound for a more effective resolution (just like the V7/III and V7/VI). In other words, the Mixolydian b13 changes into a Mixolydian b9,b13,#9.

## A1 Section (Diatonic Harmonization, inversions, secondary dominants and II-V cadences):

Now that we have the A section done, A1 will be much easier to harmonize since it is very similar to section A.

The melody on the first 4 measures is exactly the same as on section A, but for variation purposes, I will harmonize it slightly different. As you can see in the next image, I added a G chord with the third on the bass on measure 18, then replaced the original C/E chord with an Am7 chord on measure 19 and kept the Fmaj7 on measure 20. The chord on measure 18 provides more movement and a descending bass line (C moves to B and B moves to A).

Measure 21 and 22 was a good spot to include a II – V cadence that will resolve to the VIm7 degree (even though the melody notes remained diatonic). I made this decision to vary from the diatonic harmony sound for a moment and have a sense of tonicization to another diatonic degree. I did a similar thing on measure 24 where I placed a V7/IV (C7) with the thirteenth on the melody. This causes a very nice effect because we have a tension on the melody right after having a chord tone on the melody of the previous measure (melody note A over Am7).

Once you start including secondary dominants to a harmonic progression the direction gets slightly clearer because you start providing a harmonic expectation of resolution. That being said, the C7 will naturally resolve to an Fmaj7 chord on measure 25. On measure 26 I increased the harmonic beat by adding 2 simple diatonic chords which will lead into a II – V cadence (Am7 – D7) that should resolve to the V7 degree, but doesn't.

## 160 | Applications of Contemporary Harmony I

The D7 chord changes to a Dm7 chord instead (which sounds like a G7 should come after that in order to complete the progression and resolve to C), which eventually comes on measure 30 as the end of a turnaround. On measure 29 I included a II – V cadence to the IIm7 degree (Em7 – A7) which will then resolve to the second part of the turnaround on measure 30 (Dm7 – G7) and finally resolve to the tonic (C6).

The last measure of this section is a preparation for the B section which almost sounds like a modulation, but it's just a secondary dominant that will resolve to its corresponding diatonic degree.

Note: On an AABA tune, it is very common to have the B section on a different key (usually the relative minor or relative major) or like in this case, have the B section start on another diatonic degree with the preparation of its corresponding secondary dominant, which will sound like a tonicization of that degree, but we are still in the same key.

This is how this section looks like:

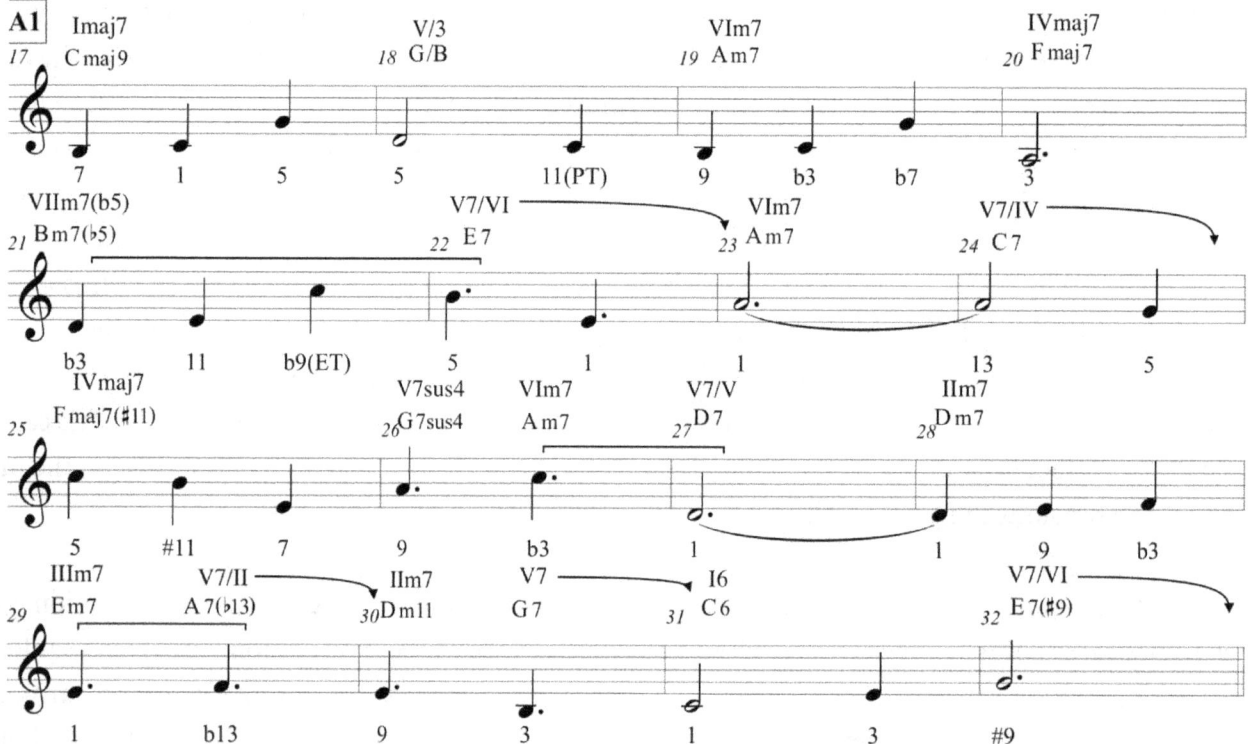

| Measure # | Chord | Function | Chord-Scale | Available Natural Tensions | Tensions Used on Melody |
|---|---|---|---|---|---|
| 17 | Cmaj9 | Imaj7 | C Ionian or C Lydian | 9, (#11), 13 | |
| 18 | G/B | V/3 | G Mixolydian | 9, (#11), 13 | |
| 19 | Am7 | VIm7 | A Aeolian | 9, 11 | 9 |
| 20 | Fmaj7 | IVmaj7 | F Lydian | 9, #11, 13 | |
| 21 | Bm7(b5) | VIIm7(b5) | B Locrian | 11 | 11 |
| 22 | E7 | V7/VI | E Mixolydian b9,b13,#9 | b9, b13, #9 | |
| 23 | Am7 | VIm7 | A Aeolian | 9, 11 | |
| 24 | C7 | V7/IV | C Mixolydian | 9, 13 | 13 |
| 25 | Fmaj7(#11) | IVmaj7 | F Lydian | 9, #11, 13 | #11 |
| 26 | -G7sus4<br>-Am7 | -V7sus4<br>-VIm7 | -G Mixolydian (Avoid 3)<br>-A Aeolian | -9, (3), 13<br>-9, 11 | -V7sus4= 9 |
| 27 | D7 | V7/V | D Mixolydian | 9, 13 | |
| 28 | Dm7 | IIm7 | D Dorian | 9, 11, (13) | 9 |
| 29 | -Em7<br>-A7(b13) | -IIIm7<br>-V7/II | -E Phrygian (Or Dorian)<br>-A Mixolydian b9,b13b#9 | -IIIm7= 9, 11<br>-V7/II= b9, b13, #9 | -V7/II= b13 |
| 30 | -Dm11<br>-G7 | -IIm7<br>-V7 | -D Dorian<br>-G Mixolydian | -IIm7= 9, 11, (13)<br>-V7= 9, (#11), 13 | -IIm7= 9 |
| 31 | C6 | I6 | | 9, (#11), 13 | |
| 32 | E7(#9) | V7 | | B9, b13, #9 | #9 |

## B Section (Diatonic Harmonization, inversions, secondary dominants and II-V cadences):

The melody of the B section of this tune contains some chromatic notes that may be chromatic non-chord tones or may be implying a secondary dominant (being either the 3rd or the 7th of the chord). The best way to qualify them is to see on what beat they are being placed. For example, on measure 33 we can see a D# on a weak beat going to an E on a strong beat; this will most likely be a chromatic non-chord tone (in this case a chromatic appoggiatura). On measure 35 we see the same note but this time it's placed on a strong beat and for a long duration (beats 1 and 2), hence this has to be a chord-tone or a chord extension. If we listen to the melodic result of the first 4 measures of the B section, we can easily determine that measures 35 and 36 are implying a B7 chord (V7/III) which resolves to Em11 (IIIm7) on measure 37.

Measure 33 could easily fit a Cmaj7 chord (Imaj7) but that wouldn't be a great decision since we would lack harmonic direction/variation. As the entire A section moves harmonically around C major, the B section would be a good spot to try to get out of that by the use of modulation (to be discussed in the next chapters) or by the use of secondary dominants and II – V cadences that might sound like we are going to another key, but still work their way around functionally back to C major.

The last measure of section A1 (measure 32) was harmonized with an E7 chord (V7/VI) which sounds like the preparation for either a modulation or a tonicization to the corresponding resolution (Am7). By ending the section on this chord, we've instantly changed the harmonic direction and we give the listener an expectation for the next section.

With an AABA tune like this one, the next section is where we need as much variation as possible in order to get away from the material exposed on the two A sections (A and A1) to avoid repetition. If we harmonize measure 32 with a G7 chord and measure 33 with a Cmaj7 chord, we would lose harmonic interest completely since it would sound like we are going back to another A section.

So far we start the B section with 2 measures of Am7 and then change to B7 with a very expressive and harmonically obvious melodic statement (measures 35 and 36).

This B7 resolves to an Em11 with the 11th on the melody as a sustained note; then I basically used that Em7 as part of a II-V cadence to the IIm7 degree by connecting it with an A9 chord. This chord resolves deceptively down a fifth to D7 (V7/II) instead of resolving to Dm7 (IIm7). The D7 changes to a Dm7, which then gets involved in a II-V cadence of the tonic chord.

Notice how from measure 37 until measure 44 we basically have tensions as the important melody notes. This was done on purpose in order to create more tension and add a thicker color to this section of the piece, which by nature should be more intense than the A sections.

Also notice how the melody note B is the 9th of A9 on measure 39 and then changes to the 13th of D13 on measure 41; that is a very good example of changing the color of one note during a relatively long period of time.

Measures 45 through 47 are a harmonic hint of the first 3 measures of the A section even though the melody is completely different (this is a great example of having a set of chords become a thematic element in the tune). On measure 48 we see a Bb on a strong beat for a long duration (beats 1 and 2), which means that this has to be a chord-tone or a harmonic extension.

Since I've been harmonizing the notes of the previous measures as tensions this will probably be a good time to break that and make this Bb a chord tone; therefore, I harmonized measure 48 with a II-V cadence of the IVmaj7 degree making that Bb a b3 of Gm7. This clearly resolves to an Fmaj7 chord (IVmaj7) – we can see a very effective result of that Bb resolving half a step to the melody note A on measure 49.

Measure 50 could easily stay as an Fmaj7 chord, but since we are just about to end the B section, it is more intense to have a faster harmonic rhythm. This is why I harmonized this measure with an Am7 which will also be used as part of a II-V cadence of the V7 degree (just like I've been doing earlier in this section). The last 4 measures are almost an exact melodic repetition of what just came before (except for the melody note D on measure 56), so I decided to repeat that same II-V cadence. This provides the listener with an insistent effect (I really mean this musical statement!!) and this effect works so well because it's done both melodically and harmonically.

The only difference is that the second time through, I actually resolve that D9 to a G7 in order to efficiently return to the last A section of the tune.

## 164 | Applications of Contemporary Harmony I

This is how this section looks like:

| Measure # | Chord | Function | Chord-Scale | Available Natural Tensions | Tensions Used on Melody |
|---|---|---|---|---|---|
| 33 – 34 | Am7 | VIm7 | A Aeolian | 9, 11 | 11 |
| 35 – 36 | B7 | V7/III | B Mixolydian b9, b13, #9 | b9, b13, #9 | |
| 37 – 38 | Em7 | IIIm7 | E Phrygian (or E Dorian) | 9, 11 | 11 |
| 39 – 40 | A9 | V7/II | *A Mixolydian | 9, 13 | 9 |
| 41 – 42 | D13 | V7/V | D Mixolydian | 9, 13 | 9 |
| 43 | Dm7 | IIm7 | D Dorian | 9, 11, (13) | 13 |
| 44 | G13 | V7 | G Mixolydian | 9, (#11), 13 | |
| 45 | Cmaj7(9,13) | Imaj7 | C Ionian or C Lydian | 9 (#11), 13 | 9, 13 |
| 46 | G/B | V/3 | G Mixolydian | 9, (#11), 13 | |
| 47 | Am7 | VIm7 | A Aeolian | 9, 11 | 9 |
| 48 | -Gm7 <br> -C7 | -V7/IV | -Gm7= G Dorian <br> -V7/IV= C Mixolydian | -Gm7= 9,11 <br> -V7/IV= 9, 13 | |
| 49 | Fmaj7 | IVmaj7 | F Lydian | 9, #11, 13 | |
| 50 | Am7 | VIm7 | A Aeolian | 9, 11 | 9 |
| 51 – 52 | D9 | V7/V | D Mixolydian | 9, 13 | 9 |
| 53 – 54 | Am7 | VIm7 | A Aeolian | 9, 11 | 9 |
| 55 | D9 | V7/V | D Mixolydian | 9, 13 | 9 |
| 56 | G7 | V7 | G Mixolydian | 9, (#11), 13 | |

Finally, we get to the last A section (A2) which is almost the same as A1 with the exception of some melodic changes and some reharmonization applied:

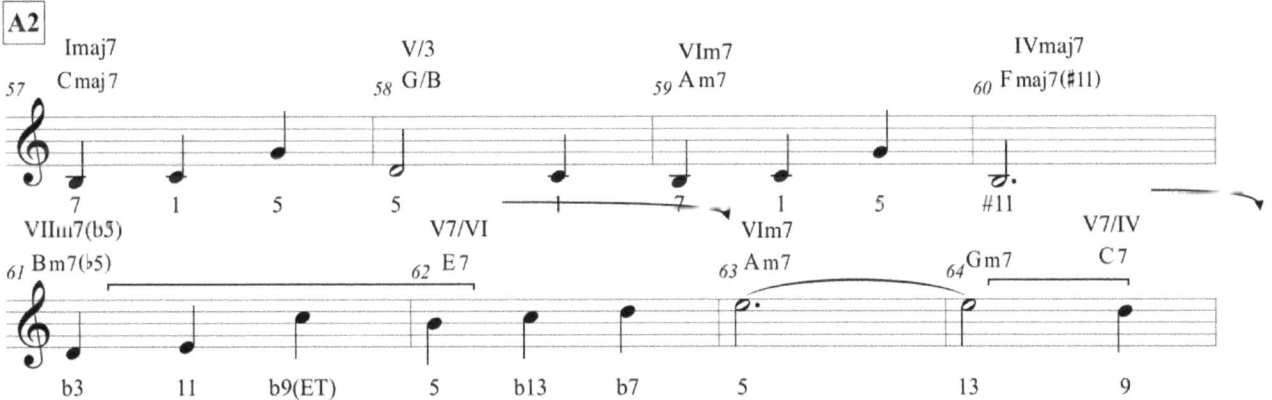

166 | *Applications of Contemporary Harmony I*

In this first part of section A2, we can see that the only thing that differentiates this section from A1 is that on measure 62 the melody keeps moving up until that note E instead of going down like before. This makes this section sound a lot more climactic and as result it gives the effect that the tune is just about to end. Because of this, the harmony has to help the climax by either increasing its harmonic rhythm and/or by using certain chords that will move the harmonic direction a lot faster and more drastically, in order to reinforce the feeling that the end is about to arrive. In this case, I simply added a II-V cadence to the IVmaj7 degree (Gm7 – C7) on measure 64.

NOTE: Section A1 only had C7 in that same spot.

The next part of Section A2 contains the exact same harmonic progression as section A1, with a slight melody change that will imply an ending to the tune:

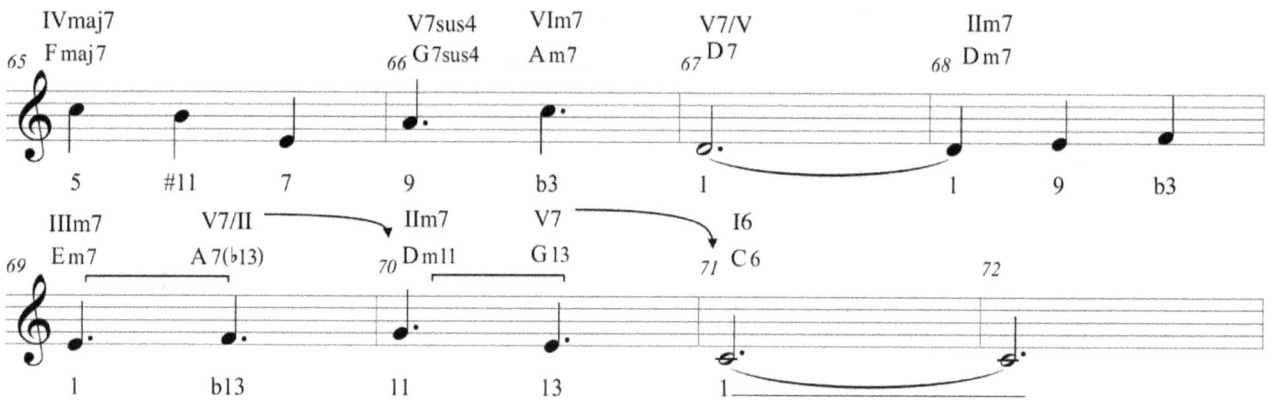

Now, let's take a look at how everything looks like...

## Reharm Waltz

Lorenzo Ferrero

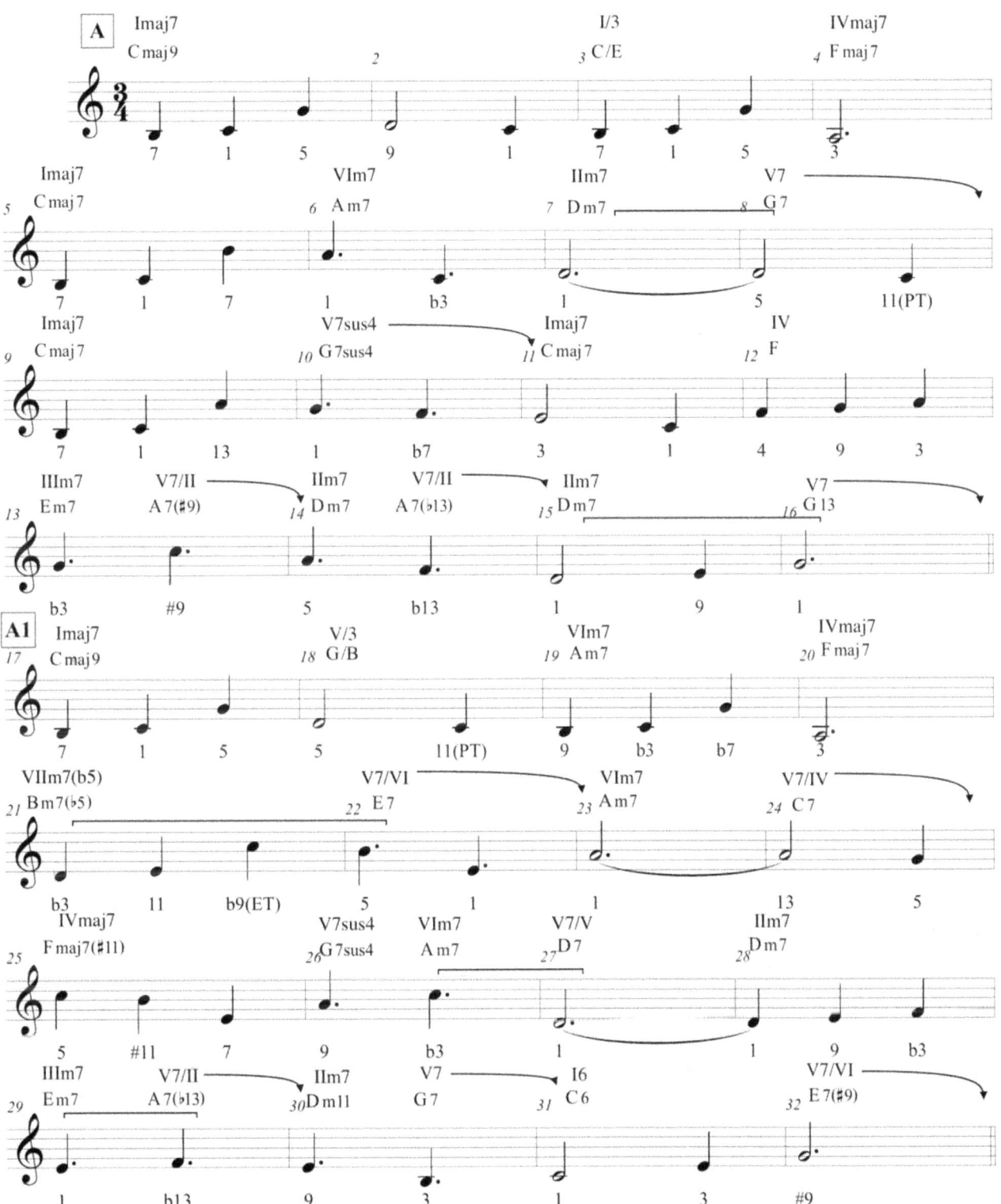

# Applications of Contemporary Harmony I

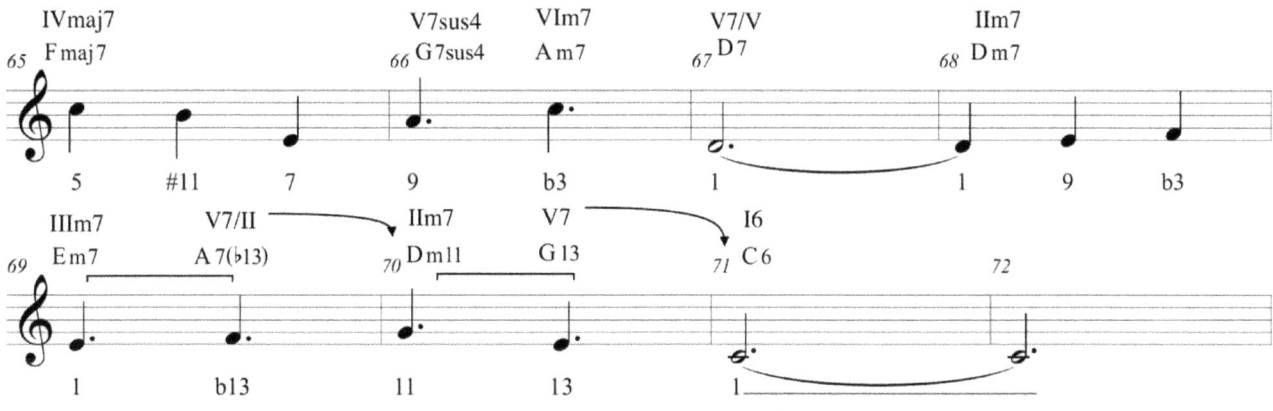

# [7] Modulation

MODULATION is the art of changing from one key to another within the same piece of music. This can be done by many different techniques, but in this book we will only cover the basic modulation techniques.

Modulation can happen around any key relationship but it is most common to modulate within the keys that are closest in relation to the circle of fifths. For example, a song in C major could modulate to F major or G major. It is also common to modulate to the relative minor key. Again, in the case of C major, it would be A minor.

This table contains the closest related keys to five major tonalities and their relative minor tonalities: C major and A minor, G major and E minor, F major and D minor, D major and B minor, Bb major and G minor.

Applications of Contemporary Harmony I

R.M= Relative minor

| Home Keys | Closest related keys to the right in order (up fifths) | Closest related keys to the left in order (down fifths) |
|---|---|---|
| C Major | G Major, D Major, A Major | F Major, Bb Major, Eb Major/D# Major |
| R.M: A minor | E minor, B minor, F# minor/Gb minor | D minor, G minor, C minor |
| G major | D Major, A Major, E Major | C Major, F Major, Bb Major |
| R.M: E minor | B minor, F# minor, C# minor/Db minor | A minor, D minor, G minor |
| F Major | C Major, G Major, D Major | Bb Major, Eb Major/D# Major, Ab Major |
| R.M: D minor | A minor, E minor, B minor | G minor, C minor, F minor |
| D Major | A Major, E Major, B Major | G Major, C Major, F Major |
| R.M: B minor/Cb minor | F# minor/Gb minor, C# minor/Db minor, G# minor/Ab minor | E minor/D# minor, A minor, D minor |
| Bb Major | F Major, C Major, G Major | Eb Major/D# Major, Ab Major, Db Major/C# Major |
| R.M: G minor | D minor, A minor, E minor | C minor, F minor, Bb minor |

There are many different types of modulations; some are more common in classical music practice, others in Jazz and other contemporary music styles. In this chapter we will cover the basic types of modulation.

- Diatonic Pivot Modulation:

This is one of the most common types of modulation, which is based on modulating by the use of a common diatonic chord between the two tonalities (the original key and the destination key). For example, if we are in C major and we want to modulate to G major, we have 3 common diatonic chords between the two keys; these can be used as *pivot chords*: Cmaj7, Em7 and Am7. So any of these 3 chords can be used to smoothly modulate from one key to the other.

When analyzing pivot modulation, we have to first identify the pivot chord(s), which will be located right before we start seeing chords that are not diatonic to the original key. Let's take a look at a short example of a musical phrase in C major, which will modulate to G major using some diatonic pivot chords:

Right when the modulation starts or when the pivot chord starts (in this case on measure 4), we write down the name of the new key and we analyze the pivot chord(s) both in the original key and in the new key.

As you can see in the example above, the pivot chords contain two different analyses: The one from the original key and the one from the new key. In this case our diatonic pivot chords are Em7 and Cmaj7 (Am7 could also be a pivot chord but analyzing that in G major would be going too far behind). Another thing to consider when analyzing is the actual sonic effect of the modulation. Sometimes, when reading a musical piece, the modulation may appear to happen early but when you actually hear it, it doesn't sound like a modulation until much later. Also, C major and G major share quite a few common chords so the exact place of the first pivot chord can become ambiguous.

Something to consider as well is if there is an alteration in the melody that could imply another key. In the case of the example above, we see an F# in the melody of measure 6 which already implies the key of G major.

Another very common diatonic pivot modulation is when a major tonality modulates to its relative minor or the other way around.

Let's see how a tune in a minor key modulates to its relative major.

The following example is in G minor and contains diatonic chords and secondary dominants. The modulation is happening at the end of the second system where we can see a II-V cadence to Bb major, which is the corresponding relative major.

- Chromatic Pivot Modulation

This type of modulation is also based on common chords between the two tonalities, but in this case the pivot chord will contain a chromatic note (non-diatonic) that will make the transition from one key to the other more colorful. The most common use of a chromatic pivot chord is to use a secondary dominant, which instead of resolving to the corresponding diatonic degree, will resolve to the new key. For example, if we are in the key of C major and we want to modulate to G major, we can use a D7 chord (V7/V). However, instead of resolving to G7, it will resolve to Gmaj7, which has nothing to do with C major anymore. It has become a modulation:

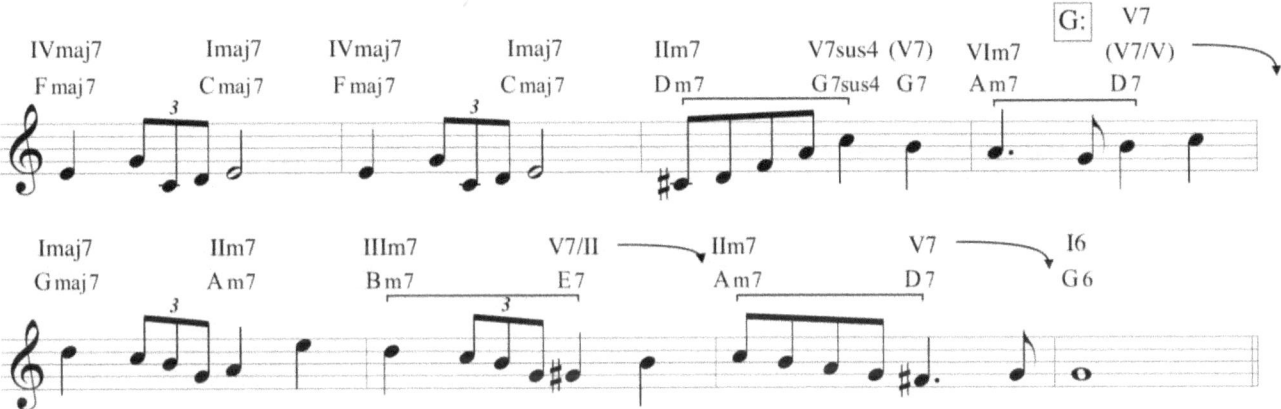

- Direct Modulation

As the name implies, this is a type of modulation that happens abruptly without any pivot that could make the modulation smoother. A direct modulation is not very aggressive when modulating to a key close in the circle of fifths, since even if there is no pivot suggested, the harmonic progression will have some chords that belong to both tonalities. This type of modulation has the most impact when modulating to a key farther in the circle of fifths; in other words, when it modulates to a key that has no diatonic chords in common with the original key.

Let's take a look at a simple harmonic progression based on moving around the II-V cadences of G major and then modulating to C major:

The form of this example is clearly "AB" with a repetition. The A section is in G major and the modulation happens right at the beginning of the B section where we can see a complete repetition of the A section (without the last chord), this time in C major.

This progression is a little tricky since the modulation doesn't happen in the Imaj7 chord of the destination key, but happens on the IIm7. It is important to understand the functions in every tonality in order to identify and/or apply the modulation techniques using any set of chords from the new tonality, not just the Imaj7 chord, this will also make the modulation more interesting.

Most of these modulations happen without a key signature change since they only happen for a short period of time and usually between closely related keys.

Sometimes, when modulating to distant keys, it is better to include a key signature change in order to avoid an overuse of accidentals in the melody.

Applications of Contemporary Harmony I | 177

The example below is a short melody that starts in Bb major and then modulates directly to G major with the inclusion of a key signature change:

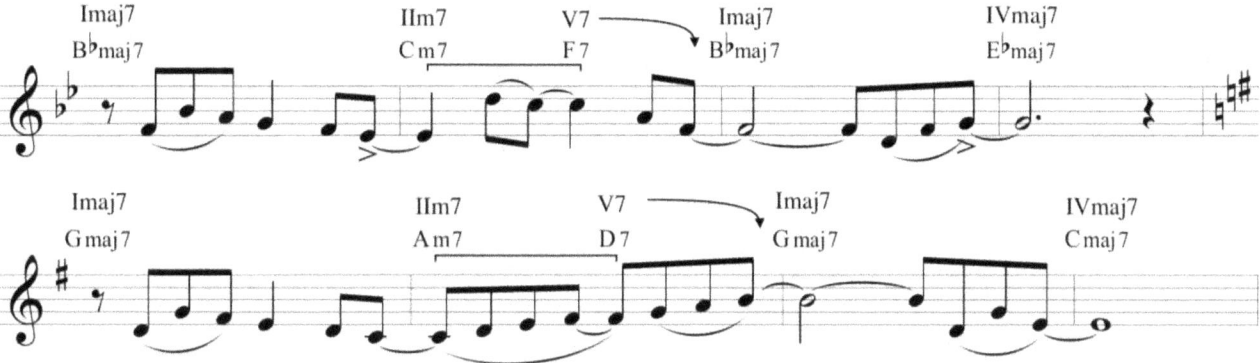

This last example demonstrates an efficient use of pivot and direct modulation into closely related keys. The form of the song is ABA:

# How It Used To Be

As you can see in the image above, the song is in C major and it modulates to G major and later on to Bb major. Both keys are closely related in the circle of fifths (G major is one key to the right, and Bb major is two keys to the left)

The following table contains a breakdown of the pivot modulations from the previous image:

| Measure # where the modulation happens | Pivot Chord/s | Current Key | Functional analysis in the current key | New Key (Destination Key) | Functional analysis in the new (destination) key |
| --- | --- | --- | --- | --- | --- |
| 5 | Am7 – D7 | C Major | VIm7 – V7/V | G Major | IIm7 – V7 |
| 7 | A7(b13) | G Major | V7/V | C Major | V7/II |
| 15 | NO PIVOT | C Major | | Bb Major | |
| 17 | G7 | Bb Major | V7/II | C Major | V7 |
| 20 | Am9 – D7 | C Major | VIm7 – V7/V | G Major | IIm7 – V7 |
| 22 | A7(b13) | G Major | V7/V | C Major | V7/II |

Notice that the modulation that happens on measure 15 (from C major to Bb major) is considered to be a direct modulation even though the chords from the previous measure (Gm7 – C13) are both analyzable in Bb major. This is because acoustically, you don't really hear the modulation until the Cm7 chord since that is the chord that takes us away from C major. In this context, Gm7 and C13 are implying a II-V cadence to the IVmaj7 degree and they don't sound like VIm7 – V7/V, which is the functional analysis in Bb major.

It is vital that these concepts are practiced continuously in order to continue developing your musical abilities and increasingly be able to recognize the function of a chord in any given tonality, so that manipulate a harmonic progression becomes a piece of cake. This is a very long process and it requires a lot of application and consistency to achieve.

This is a good exercise that I've used throughout my years of practice that serves as a mind game/workout of functional harmony:

1. Pick any chord. (E.g.: Am7, Cmaj7, E7, Abm7(b5), Gm7, etc.)
2. After picking your chord, think about any tonality. Try picking a key that could possibly contain the selected chord.
3. Identify the function that your selected chord has in your selected tonality.
4. Select a different tonality and identify the new function of the chord you originally selected. (This step should be done several times in order to start familiarizing the functionality of the selected chord in different tonalities)

**Example #1:**

1. Pick a chord: Cmaj7
2. Pick Tonality: G Major
3. Identify the chord's function within the selected tonality: Cmaj7 is IVmaj7 in G major
4. Select a different tonality and identify the chord's new function:

- Cmaj7 is Imaj7 in C major

**Example #2**

1. Pick a chord: E7
2. Pick Tonality: D Major
3. Identify the chord's function within the selected tonality: E7 is V7/V in D major
4. Select a different tonality and identify the chord's new function:

- E7 is V7/III in F major
- E7 is V7/VI in C major
- E7 is V7/II in G major
- E7 is V7 in A major and A minor
- E7 is bVII7 in F# minor

As you can see in the image above, the song is in C major and it modulates to G major and later on to Bb major. Both keys are closely related in the circle of fifths (G major is one key to the right, and Bb major is two keys to the left)

The following table contains a breakdown of the pivot modulations from the previous image:

| Measure # where the modulation happens | Pivot Chord/s | Current Key | Functional analysis in the current key | New Key (Destination Key) | Functional analysis in the new (destination) key |
|---|---|---|---|---|---|
| 5 | Am7 – D7 | C Major | VIm7 – V7/V | G Major | IIm7 – V7 |
| 7 | A7(b13) | G Major | V7/V | C Major | V7/II |
| 15 | NO PIVOT | C Major |  | Bb Major |  |
| 17 | G7 | Bb Major | V7/II | C Major | V7 |
| 20 | Am9 – D7 | C Major | VIm7 – V7/V | G Major | IIm7 – V7 |
| 22 | A7(b13) | G Major | V7/V | C Major | V7/II |

Notice that the modulation that happens on measure 15 (from C major to Bb major) is considered to be a direct modulation even though the chords from the previous measure (Gm7 – C13) are both analyzable in Bb major. This is because acoustically, you don't really hear the modulation until the Cm7 chord since that is the chord that takes us away from C major. In this context, Gm7 and C13 are implying a II-V cadence to the IVmaj7 degree and they don't sound like VIm7 – V7/V, which is the functional analysis in Bb major.

It is vital that these concepts are practiced continuously in order to continue developing your musical abilities and increasingly be able to recognize the function of a chord in any given tonality, so that manipulate a harmonic progression becomes a piece of cake. This is a very long process and it requires a lot of application and consistency to achieve.

This is a good exercise that I've used throughout my years of practice that serves as a mind game/workout of functional harmony:

1. Pick any chord. (E.g.: Am7, Cmaj7, E7, Abm7(b5), Gm7, etc.)
2. After picking your chord, think about any tonality. Try picking a key that could possibly contain the selected chord.
3. Identify the function that your selected chord has in your selected tonality.
4. Select a different tonality and identify the new function of the chord you originally selected. (This step should be done several times in order to start familiarizing the functionality of the selected chord in different tonalities)

**Example #1:**

1. Pick a chord: Cmaj7
2. Pick Tonality: G Major
3. Identify the chord's function within the selected tonality: Cmaj7 is IVmaj7 in G major
4. Select a different tonality and identify the chord's new function:

- Cmaj7 is Imaj7 in C major

**Example #2**

1. Pick a chord: E7
2. Pick Tonality: D Major
3. Identify the chord's function within the selected tonality: E7 is V7/V in D major
4. Select a different tonality and identify the chord's new function:

- E7 is V7/III in F major
- E7 is V7/VI in C major
- E7 is V7/II in G major
- E7 is V7 in A major and A minor
- E7 is bVII7 in F# minor

Keep doing this with any other chord and key selection. The options are limited if we only consider the concepts discussed in "Applications of Contemporary Harmony I" but they will become endless after the concepts that will be discussed in the second book.

Modulation is essential to music; it brings mobility and freshness to a harmonic progression; it is the main musical source to provide variation.

As the great French composer Charles-Henri Blainville said:

*"Modulation is the essential part of the art. Without it there is little music, for a piece derives its true beauty not from the large number of fixed modes which it embraces but rather from the subtle fabric of its modulation"*

In *"Applications of Contemporary Harmony II"*, we will extend this topic and include all the possibilities of modulation used in contemporary music.

## Preview and Topics for "Applications of Contemporary Harmony II"

*"Applications of Contemporary Harmony II"* will expand the topics of this book and will introduce many new topics regarding functional harmony. The second part of this book will contain non-functional harmony and some composition techniques. Most importantly, it will explain how to use certain harmonic techniques melodically and it will further expand the possibilities of reharmonization.

These are some of the topics that will be covered on the book:

- Modal Interchange
- Diminished Chords
- Extended, Substitute and special function Dominants
- Advanced Modulation
- Harmonization and Reharmonization 3
- Chord Scale Voicings. Advanced Harmonic and Melodic Application
- Upper Structure Triads and Hybrid Chords
- Modal Harmony
- Non-Functional Harmony – Constant Structures
- Harmonization and Reharmonization 4

## Some last words for the reader

With "Applications of Contemporary Harmony I" you will be able to understand basic functional harmony in the modern music world and use the concepts thoroughly in order to be able to analyze, arrange, reharmonize and compose music.

Always remember that these concepts, when used for harmonizing or reharmonizing, should be applied consciously in order to have a clear harmonic direction and to avoid an overuse of chords that will result too intense and complicated. On the other hand, these concepts will help you bring life and color to simple songs in any genre and will help you make more efficient decisions when struggling trying to find what the next chord of your song should be.

Harmony is a consequence of form and direction; so it is extremely important to know what your destination is going to be in order to write an efficient chord progression. After studying the next book, *"Applications of Contemporary Harmony II"*, you will have all the tools needed to fully understand and apply advanced contemporary harmony into any style of music and your mind will become a lot faster in processing musical information.

Proficient harmonic knowledge is fundamental in order to work as a composer, arranger, conductor, producer, musical director, etc. It will eventually give you such a great understanding of musical functions that you will have a broader and unique perspective, with a set of tools that will expand all the possibilities you have with music. You will be able to transpose a piece of music on the spot, compose a lot faster, improvise with your main instrument proficiently, and it will give you a broader understanding and identify what concepts fit within each style of music. It is absolutely important that you listen to different styles of music as much as possible; especially music where a lot of thought, technique and soul has been poured into. It can be classical music, Jazz, R&B, Funk or Soul to mention a few. Try to analyze how the harmonic progressions work for each of these styles and transcribe as many songs as possible as an exercise.

Little by little, almost without noticing, you will start developing your own harmonic vocabulary which will contain certain concepts that you like, things that you've heard and transcribed over the years, and new approaches that you might come up with. This will hopefully give your music a color that no one else has.

# Index

Appoggiatura, 31
Cadence, 12, 13, 14, 116, 118
Chord, 2, 30, 42, 47, 53, 68, 79, 105, 106, 107, 108, 109, 123, 130, 132, 138, 158, 161, 165
Comping, 25
Diatonic, 76, 77
Dominant Function, 5, 19, 42, 47, 49, 101, 104
Downbeat, 51
Escape tones, 30, 32
Guide tones, 86
Harmonic beat, 7
Harmonization, 39, 45, 155
Inversion, 11, 26
Modes, 28
Modulation, 90
Musical Period, 8
Neighbor tones, 30, 32
Non-Chord tones, 30

Parallel minor key, 104
Passing tones, 30, 32, 33
Reharmonization, 7, 41, 48, 49, 139
Relative minor key, 104
Retardation, 31
Retardations, 33
Secondary dominants, 57, 59, 60, 61, 64, 65, 67, 68, 69, 70, 71, 72, 74, 75, 78, 79, 81, 82, 132, 148, 159, 162
Seventh chord, 18, 21, 24, 56, 57, 64, 71, 72, 73, 74
Sub-Dominant Function, 5, 19, 47, 49
Suspension, 31
Tetrachord, 102
Tonic Function, 4, 9, 19, 42, 47, 49
Triads, 11, 2, 3, 4, 20, 56
Tri-tone, 56
Upbeat, 51
Voice leading, 27
Weak Beat, 51

# References

Felts, R. (2002) Reharmonization Techniques
    Boston, Massachusetts: Berklee Press

Pease, T. & Pullig, K. (2001) Modern Jazz Voicings
    Boston, Massachusetts: Berklee Press

Pease. T. (2003) – Jazz Composition Theory and Practice
    Boston, Massachusetts: Berklee Press

## ABOUT THE AUTHOR

LORENZO FERRERO is a renowned saxophonist, composer, arranger and educator. He started playing the Clarinet at the age of 13 and soon joined the Peruvian Youth National Orchestra. At the age of 16 he discovered the tenor saxophone and it became his primary instrument. During the following years, he started taking lessons in Jazz improvisation and theory. In 2009 he attended Berklee College of Music on a scholarship where he majored in Jazz composition, orchestration and orchestral conducting. After graduating Magna Cum Laude, he moved to Vienna to perform on a European tour as a band member of renowned bassist Juan Garcia Herreros, "Snow Owl".

During his time in Austria, Lorenzo also worked as a session saxophonist, collaborating with the top musicians of the country. He recorded several projects with Grammy Award winner Georg Luksch and was commissioned by the University of Technology of Vienna to write the opening waltz for the ceremony commemorating the 200 anniversary of their annual ball, which was held on January 2015. Lorenzo became a part of Musketier Music Agency in Austria, where he continues to work as a freelance arranger, producer and composer for several musical projects including being musical director of the album "Love is Alive" by renowned singer Ola Egbowon.

In 2014, Lorenzo founded the "Jazz and Contemporary Music Workshops", a program created with the purpose of bringing contemporary music knowledge to the young musicians of his hometown Lima, Peru. Since then, he has been invited to teach several clinics at different institutions, including the National Conservatory of Music in Lima and The University of San Martin de Porres, among others.

Lorenzo has performed in many countries throughout the world including the United States, Canada, Austria, Germany, Slovakia, Greece, Peru and Italy. He relocated to Los Angeles in November 2015. Since then, he has worked as lead assistant to renowned Hollywood composer Christopher Young, and continues to perform with world-renowned musicians. He is a member of the band *"Alex Acuña and 7 bien"* and has formed his own big band alongside Peruvian saxophonist Anibal Seminario, where he continues to expand his expertise by conducting, arranging and performing with the band. Additionally, he has become an author after being published by the music publishing company *"Violet Anamnesis"* with his books: *"Applications of Contemporary Harmony vol. I"* and *"Applications of Contemporary Harmony, vol. II"*

His most influential teachers include *George Garzone, Frank Tiberi, Dennis Leclair, Greg Hopkins, Yakov Gubanov, Conrad Pope and Christopher Young*. He has also performed with international acclaimed artists such as *Arturo Sandoval, Alex Acuña, Ramon Stagnaro, Oscar Stagnaro, Otmaro Ruiz, Juan Garcia Herreros (Snow Owl), Hector Martignon, Roberto Quintero and Carlo Mombelli*, among others.